THE BOYS OF BRADDOCK

ANDREW CARNEGIE AND THE MEN WHO CHANGED INDUSTRIAL HISTORY

QUENTIN R. SKRABEC, JR., PH.D.

HERITAGE BOOKS
2006

HERITAGE BOOKS
AN IMPRINT OF HERITAGE BOOKS, INC.

Books, CDs, and more—Worldwide

For our listing of thousands of titles see our website
at
www.HeritageBooks.com

Cover illustration of nineteenth-century Bessemer furnace from
United States Steel, 1951 Anniversary Edition
Courtesy of United States Steel Corporation

Published 2006 by
HERITAGE BOOKS, INC.
Publishing Division
65 East Main Street
Westminster, Maryland 21157-5026

Copyright © 2004 Quentin R. Skrabec, Jr., Ph.D.

All rights reserved. No part of this book may be reproduced or transmitted in any form or by any means, electronic or mechanical, including photocopying, recording or by any information storage and retrieval system without written permission from the author, except for the inclusion of brief quotations in a review.

International Standard Book Number: 978-0-7884-2516-1

To Our Lady of Loretto
Patroness of Braddock

and

My Daughter Diane

Table of Contents

Introduction vii

A Wilderness Crossing 1

Braddock's Field 19

Iron Comes to the Valley 33

The Sleepy Village Awakes 51

"ET"—Edgar Thomson Works 65

Captain Bill Jones 79

Charles Schwab: The Steel Titan 105

The Steel Town of Braddock 141

The Boys of Braddock 159

The Industrial Edwardians 181

Experiments in Industrial Management 197

Carnegie Veterans Association 207

Bibliography 217

Index 219

Introduction

The town of Braddock today remains lost, according to most American history books. The battlefields of Gettysburg, Lexington, Bull Run, Bunker Hill, Antietam, and others are national treasures. But the battlefield that once was known throughout Europe as a turning point in history has been reduced to a few hard-to-find markers. The Battle of Braddock that launched the great career of George Washington has been reduced to American trivia. The spirit of the events, however, is clearly traceable.

The very industry and country that Braddock played so much a part in building have deserted it. The thousands of steelworkers who lost their lives in forging American industry lay forgotten. The steel that was produced the in the Monongahela valley resulted in winning World War II and launched America as the supreme industrial center and a political super power. The proud spirit of this unique geographic point of American history is broken today. The mythical folk hero of the town, Joe Magarac, lies resting somewhere in the hills above the town. The very industry that was so protected by our politicians in the nineteenth century as the core of our economic success has been left to rust. The grandsons of those steelworkers who benefited from the libraries that Big Steel built have moved on to other careers and towns. Great buildings have been lost. Even today's residents know little of the town's glorious past.

Still, the past has shown that such great historical centers commonly rise again. It is a spirit that haunts these great locations. This book is about that spirit and Braddock's legacy. The history of the town of Braddock is as rich as that of most great cities. Maybe more importantly, it is central to the very history of our great nation.

Braddock's Edgar Thomson Steel Works still stands today. What few realize is that this steel plant could be classified as one of the Industrial Revolution's wonders of the world. It goes far beyond the legacy of Andrew Carnegie and United States Steel Corporation. Braddock was the think tank of the Industrial Revolution. It pioneered industrial chemistry, industrial technology and integrated process control. Its greatest contribution, however, was in the field of industrial management. Braddock would birth a group of managers that would change American industry. The concepts these managers would develop are in many cases just starting to come to full application. The story is a true genealogy of nineteenth and twentieth-century industrial managers.

Another part of the story is the bonding and friendship, which started in Braddock, that would carry these managers for many decades. They were bound by a philosophy and a dream for American industry.

The time period of Braddock's industrial history spans parts of two centuries but fits well historically and intellectually with the Victorian and Edwardian eras. It also allows for a method to distinguish between the great believers and inventors of industrial technology such as Andrew Carnegie, Henry Clay Frick, Henry Bessemer and Alexander Holly and the managerial humanists such as the "boys of Braddock." The Industrial Victorians were the earliest movers of the Industrial Revolution. Like Carnegie, these Industrial Victorians saw and applied science to the future. The later part of the Industrial Revolution in Braddock gave birth to the believers of finding harmony in the human and machine elements. It was this belief that allowed for the advance of the science of management.

The term "boys of Braddock," referring to a group of Edgar Thomson Works "graduates," was coined in the 1890s by the Pittsburgh press. The boys were a very close group of Carnegie employees who remained friends and associates throughout their diversified careers. At least four of the boys, Alva Dinkey, William Dickson, Charles Schwab and William Corey were boyhood friends in Braddock. The full set of boys included another ten or so Carnegie employees who were bonded in philosophy and training to Bill Jones, who was Carnegie's great plant manager of Edgar

Thomson Works. In the first two decades of the nineteenth century the boys controlled three of the largest ten American corporations as well as a handful of the next twenty-five companies. They were involved in the formation of many of today's industrial giants such as International Nickel and United States Steel Corporation, controlling as much as half of America's industrial wealth. Such a league of powerful industrialists today would be considered a conspiracy by its very existence.

Chapter One

"What kind of character is hereafter to rise from an amalgamation of such discordant material, I am at a loss to conjecture."
—*(Description of the Monongahela valley, 1806)*

A Wilderness Crossing

The genealogy of the borough of Braddock includes ancestors from at least two ancient civilizations, four Indian nations, France, England, and the United States. The Indian nations included the Iroquois, Shawnee, Delaware and Susquehannock. It has also been claimed by three states: Pennsylvania, Virginia and Maryland. Early names for the general area of Braddock included Monongahela country, Cumberland and Fort Machault. These early claims led to an unusual early mix of French, German, Irish and Scottish settlers. This original ethnic mix can still be heard in the unique nasal accent of present day residents.

Early history is the DNA of cities. It represents the past and defines the future. History reveals the spirit of a place. Even in towns like Braddock the early roots are still to be seen in the town's culture and future. The Indians talked of geographic locations as having a unique spirit. It was this protective spirit that the Indians attributed to George Washington's ability to dodge bullets in the battle of Braddock's Field. It was a spirit found in the mythical hero of Braddock, Joe Magarac. Later immigrants from southern Europe believed every city and town had its own guardian angel that embodied this spirit.

Braddock's past was a process leading to the founding of our nation, American industry, America's steel industry, and provided a model for the world's libraries. To illustrate, here is a statement by historian George Lamb on the 150th anniversary the battle of Braddock: "Braddock's Field is one of the very important localities in American history. There are few places and few incidents that may be termed pivotal, perhaps not more than seven in the whole range of United States history.... Chronologically these events associated with their localities are: Jamestown, Plymouth Rock, Braddock's Field, Lexington, Independence Hall, Saratoga, Gettysburg."[1] Braddock more than anything else has been a training ground for our nation's quest as a country and industrial giant. Braddock today remains a battlefield; however, today it is a battlefield of economic change. Still the monolithic plant of Edgar Thomson Works stands today as a functioning tribute to America's industrial history, success and challenges.

The borough of Braddock is located on an ancient oxbow flood plain of the Monongahela River. The early settlers noted the distinctive muddy yellow color of the Monongahela. This muddy color of suspended red and yellow clays is still in evidence today. The Monongahela is an Indian name, which means "high banks breaking off and falling down at places." Locals pronounce it, "Menaungehilla" which goes back to the early settlers' corruption of the Indian name. The plain on which present day Braddock is located is on the east side of the oxbow bend of the river just after the deep gorge of the entering Turtle Creek. The point of the entrance of Turtle Creek into the Monongahela is roughly ten miles upstream from the headwaters of the Ohio River at present day Pittsburgh. This flood plain at the Braddock plateau was ideal for Indian corn and rye as well as offering flat land for settlement. Although the Indians preferred to farm the flats, they housed themselves in the hills above. The entrance of the Youghiogheny River into the Monongahela a few miles upstream and the cutting power of Turtle Creek supplied an

---

[1] George H. Lamb, editor, *The Unwritten History of Braddock's Field* (Pittsburgh: Nicholson Printing, 1917), 7

ample source of sand to build these flats. Still today on the Braddock industrial landings, heavy dredging is required to keep the docks open to barge traffic. In addition this fertile plateau is enriched every spring with great floods from the nearby mountain system. This fertile plateau, coupled with the perfect place to ford the river, would define the destiny of today's Braddock.

The Monongahela, Allegheny and Ohio River systems have always been prone to flooding. The highest recorded flood level was the great flood of 1936. The great St. Patrick's Day flood of the 1930s was immortalized by the old Kennywood Amusement Park ride, "Noah's Ark." Early settlers recorded great floods in 1756, 1762 and 1763. These floods occurred in the spring as the mountains fed the river systems with melted snow. These floods were another reason the Indians always built their long houses in the hills above the river. Even today, Edgar Thomson Works often suffers from the spring flooding of the Monongahela.

The Monongahela still remains a swift dangerous river. Many eighteenth-century explorers to western Pennsylvania such as George Washington made note of that swiftness. One of the local legends tells of the existence of an underground river, underneath the Monongahela. The legend was strengthened by a crash of a B-25 bomber in the river in 1956 that was never found. The point of the crash is downriver from Braddock at a place called Bird's landing. Several attempts in 1995 and 1997 failed again to find the plane.

The wildlife of the area was much different in the 1700s. First of all the "wood" buffalo were common and were an excellent source of food and skins. The wood buffalo differed from plains buffalo in that it was larger, darker in color and lacked the hump of its plains cousin. The wood buffalo is truly extinct (unlike its plains cousin) with the last herd in the Monongahela valley reported in the 1790s. Bears, elk, deer and wolves were extremely common as well. Today the elk and wolves are gone but deer are still found and once in awhile there is a visit of a wandering bear from the mountains. Early settlers also noted panthers and wildcats. The prime fur-bearing animals such as beaver, otter and mink were not abundant in the area. Gray squirrels (as well as the usual black phase) were common, as they are now. Rats were not native to the area, and Indian legend has it that rats always appeared prior to the white man and were considered a bad omen. One Delaware legend has it that a rat first appeared prior to the white man's landing on the North American continent. Turkeys were a common food source. A large variety of other game birds were present, such as the passenger pigeon (now extinct), partridges, quail and grouse, all of which are no longer found in the area.

The now extinct passenger pigeon would darken the skies of Braddock in the eighteenth and nineteenth centuries, long before the smoke of the steel mills cast its pallor. In 1811, a traveler noted, "For short periods countless numbers of passenger pigeons blackened the skies by day and mutilated the forests by night." These flocks were miles long and miles wide, and would take hours to pass overhead. One hunter could kill tens of thousand birds in a few hours. The passenger pigeon was an excellent food source and would be abundant in Braddock into the 1860s. The last known passenger pigeon in the area was reported in the early 1870s. It should also be noted that it was in this part of western Pennsylvania that John Audubon did his famous bird print of a passenger pigeon in the 1820s.

Birds not useful for food included the bald eagle, Carolina parakeet (now extinct), the golden eagle and vultures. It is interesting to note that crows, which are now common in the area, were not native to the Monongahela valley but came with the advance of civilization. The Monongahela River was rich in perch, sturgeon, catfish, pike and bullheads. Copperheads and rattlesnakes were common, requiring the use of leather leggings by the early settlers for protection.

The most complained-about animal was the mosquito. A 1750 visitor to the area noted: "the stinging flies and divers other insects but particularly Muskeetose in this are like to rival the Seven Plagues of Egypt." Many traders of the time also noted the lack of honeybees in the area, which the Indians called the white man's flies.

The foliage was different then as well. Black walnut was common and was used in early building. Hickory was another important wood of the area, which was more elastic than walnut and found applications in tools and equipment such as wagon parts. Hickory was common around the present site of Edgar Thomson Works.[2] In fact, prior to the establishment of the mill, that site had a large grove of hickory trees and was a favorite play area of local children. Hickory was the preferred wood to produce charcoal for iron-making furnaces, but iron ore did not exist in sufficient quantity for an iron industry to fully develop in the area. Oak varieties were also common in the area and were widely used in buildings. Local oak would also be the source for the first manufactory—a barrel making plant. Chestnut was used to produce charcoal for blacksmithing and early iron production. The area had a wide variety of wild berries. Ginseng was also natural to the area and was used as a medicine and trade product. Ginseng can still be found today in some rural areas.

Another natural product of the area was coal. Coal was noted early on by scouts such as Christopher Gist in 1749. Mining of this coal across the river from Pittsburgh was occurring in 1760. The coal of the Monongahela valley fueled the later glass and steel industries. In fact it is coal that gave the name "steel valley" to the area. Iron ores, while present in

---

[2] ibid., 19

the Monongahela valley, were not available in great enough amounts to drive a modern steel industry. Because coal is so light compared to dense iron ore, it made economic sense to ship the heavy iron ore to the coalfields versus the other way. The weight in coal might require three railroad cars versus one for the iron ore. This is the reason the ore is brought over 1100 miles to the fuel in Pittsburgh and Braddock.

Coal was also a source of home heating. As late as the 1930s Depression years, Braddock residents turned to mining their own coal for heating from the hills of North Braddock, Port Perry and the Sixth Street ravine where the "Pittsburgh seam" is exposed. During the great steel strike of 1959, a number of financially hurting strikers again dug coal from the hills to heat homes. Coal would bring big steel to the valley because of its abundance and river outcroppings. This was first noted in a letter from Christopher Gist to Lawrence Washington (the brother of George Washington) in May of 1749: "described by all of the traders as vastly rich and the banks of the river expose coals."[3] The "Pittsburgh seam" is three miles wide and over fifty miles long as it goes up the Monongahela valley.

Actually the mining of coal was the chief industry of the town of Braddock prior to 1875. Early mining started in 1840 around the present site of the Braddock cemetery and Sixth Street. Probably the earliest of these miners was Scots-Irish Thomas Dickson, the grandfather of one of the "boys of Braddock," William Dickson (future vice-president of United States Steel). These Dickson mines ran through Braddock, Braddock Hills, North Braddock and Swissvale. Another of the owners was J. B. Corey of Port Perry. J. B. Corey was the grandfather of William Corey (future President of United

---

[3] Solon J. Buck and Elizabeth Hawthorn Buck, *The Planting of Civilization in Western Pennsylvania* (Pittsburgh: University of Pittsburgh Press, 1968), 20

States Steel). Corey had developed a number of mines in the Braddock area and was considered the local mining expert. This early mining was unusual in that it used a Welsh mining technique. That was the use of "ravine dogs" to pull out the coal cars. The coal was then moved down the Monongahela River on huge barges called "joe boats." These boats were seventy-five feet long. This coal mining operation was taken over by Judge Thomas Mellon (founder of Mellon Bank and future Carnegie partner) with J. B. Corey (future partner with Henry Clay Frick) as his partner about the time of the Civil War. Even today the remnants of this early mining operation can be found all over the hills of North Braddock and Braddock Hills.

The Monongahela rock strata also contain a seam of excellent "fire clay" needed for furnace brick in iron and steel making. These clays made refractory brick, which can withstand the high heat of iron and steel making. Another critical steel making component, limestone, was also abundant. Some of this limestone is well known to residents because it is rich in fossils (ancient sea shells and animals). This stratum of limestone is called "Ames" limestone after the town in Ohio where it is most prominent. The Ames formation goes back to when the area was a warm shallow sea. Much of my youth, as well as the youthful days of Pittsburghers like Andrew Carnegie, was passed collecting a wide variety of these fossils. In fact it was these abundant fossils that sparked Carnegie's lifelong interest in paleontology. Some of this limestone was a raw material to make lime for steel making and iron making. Thomas Dickson had also built lime kilns to produce lime in the hills of North Braddock. Another mineral resource of the area was silica sand, which made the Monongahela valley the center of glass making from 1790 to 1890. Glass making thrived in the valley because of the abundance of coal as fuel and the river silica sands. Few people remember that long before the Monongahela valley was the steel valley, it was the glass valley.

Braddock, like all of western Pennsylvania, is surrounded by hills. Visitors to the area often assume that these steep hills are part of the nearby mountain system. The hills are actually part of a great plateau which rivers, creeks and runs have cut deep gorges or hollows (the local term) to define the area. The Monongahela was a meandering river, which cut out wandering valleys. The Monongahela River today is a very different river controlled by an extensive system of locks and dams, which make the river navigable to deep barge traffic. Its natural tendency to meander is controlled by civilization and industrialization on its banks. Its swift character which George Washington made note of still is evident today. In Washington's early trips to the area, he searched for the ideal point of ford on the Monongahela.

This point of ford on the Monongahela at the site of future Braddock made it part of several Indian paths and one that Washington most favored. It was a major branch of the Raystown path (Raystown is present day Bedford) going to the east and the Catawba path and Warriors path going north and south. In colonial times the use of these paths, with some English roadbuilding, formed what was known as Braddock's Road, which went from Braddock's Field to Williamsburg, Virginia. These paths have become parts of Routes 40, 30, 22, and the Pennsylvania Turnpike today. Locally both Braddock and Swissvale Avenues are part of these old Indian trails. Braddock was a fertile plain and trading post on these ancient trade routes. Corn planting on the Braddock plain may go back to the very first North Americans, the paleo-Indians.

Ownership of this fertile plain of future Braddock was fuzzy prior to the European colonization. Approximately fifteen miles from Braddock's Field is one of the oldest sites of human occupation in North America: Meadowcroft Village in Washington County. This site still holds the record for the oldest carbon dated site on the North American continent at 15,000 years ago.[4] The origin of these paleo-Indians is unclear. One theory has them coming across from Asia while another suggests an early European origin.

The earliest historical evidence of early civilization in the Braddock area was a group of mound builders known as the "Monongahela People." Mounds have been found near Braddock and the Monongahela/Youghiogheny valleys, and were studied in the 1930s.[5] These Indians seem to have been colonists from the advanced Indian civilization of the Mississippi Valley. Their villages tended to be on the hilltops but they raised corn near the riverbanks. Corn was an ideal crop for river flood plains. The flood plains were farmed extensively by the Indians in the Monongahela valley. Analysis of these ancient mounds suggests that these people were more advanced than any Indian occupation to follow. Artifacts also suggest the extensive network of trading throughout the North American continent. The occurrence of native copper artifacts suggest a strong trading network with northern Michigan, which foreshadowed today's iron ore shipping networks to the steel mills of Braddock. The most amazing mystery of the Monongahela People is their disappearance in the early sixteenth century. It is still not known what caused the loss of this highly advanced culture.

The disappearance of the Monongahela People in the 1500s left most of western Pennsylvania unoccupied for almost a century. The Six Nations Iroquois of Canada and upper New York State loosely claimed the area of Braddock. The Seneca was the Iroquois nation that was given rule of the Braddock area. The Seneca were allies of the British. The eastern

---

[4] Helen Vogt, *Westward of ye Laurall Hills* (Parsons, West Virginia: McClain Printing, 1976), 73
[5] Buck and Buck, 20

Pennsylvania tribe of the Susquehannocks also claimed the Monongahela valley. For most of the seventeenth century the Susquehannocks and the Iroquois waged what are known as the "Beaver Wars" mainly to the east of Braddock. Ultimately the Iroquois won and the Seneca took claim to the Monongahela valley. Still the area remained basically unoccupied until the eighteenth century, except for hunting parties of northern-based Iroquois.

At the beginning of the eighteenth century a migration of the eastern Delaware and the western Shawnee began. The migration was allowed and monitored by the Iroquois even though the Delaware and Shawnee were allied with the French. It was during this period that the French and English were positioning for control of the Upper Ohio, Allegheny and Monongahela valleys. While the Iroquois allowed this migration, they sent assigned chiefs to the area for political control. The Iroquois were clearly the most powerful Indian nation and one of the few Indian allies of the English. The Delaware, Shawnee and other western tribes tended to favor the French but were held in line by the Seneca. The real struggle was over control of the fur trade. For the English, the "point" of the formation of the Ohio River by the Monongahela and Allegheny Rivers was the center of control for trading.

The main Indian government was not at the point of the future Pittsburgh, but at Logstown, a few miles down the Ohio River from the "point." Logstown was a mix of many Indian tribes and was courted by both the French and the English. Logstown was a major settlement, complete with cornfields to feed its population and political chiefs to govern its social order. In the 1700s Logstown was the political capital of western Pennsylvania. It was the first destination of George Washington's visit in the 1750s. Indians coming through the area were required to stop at Logstown for approval from the Iroquois "half-kings.".

The European migration was well under way in the 1740s. The Scots, Scots-Irish and the Germans were the main immigrations into the Monongahela valley. The earliest were the Scots-Irish, but English traders from Virginia were also coming in numbers. In 1750, Ben Franklin and the Pennsylvania authorities sent cartographer Lewis Evans to spy on the Monongahela and Ohio valleys. Evans gave the following report on the sparse population: "the people are of the lowest rank and least informed, of mankind who flowed from Germany, Ireland and the gaols of Great Britain, or they are the children of such, born on the land or brought in very young and are settlers by birth and profession. Their houses were but logs and as miserable and draughty as any in Ireland."[6] The Germans tended to be more stable farmers. The French and the Scots-Irish, more than the other groups, tended to intermarry with Indians in the Monongahela valley. The French settlers felt the area was part of New France and opposed all such British immigrations. Tensions were high throughout the Monongahela valley by the start of 1750.

It was during this period of territorial disputes that George Washington made his first trip to the area in 1753 at the request of the colony of Virginia. Washington followed what was known as the Virginia path, which went through Fort Cumberland (Maryland) by way of Wills Creek and the Great Meadows, via future Braddock, to the forts on the Ohio. This old Indian trail is today known as Braddock's Road.

In late 1753 Washington visited two recent settlers on the Virginia path to future Braddock. First was the English trader, John Frazier, who had established a trading post and blacksmith's shop at the exact location of the future town of

---

[6] Leland Baldwin, *Pittsburgh–The Story of a City* (Pittsburgh, University of Pittsburgh Press, 1937), 2

Braddock in 1742, where Turtle Creek enters the Monongahela. Frazier had been forced out of his earlier location at Venango at the mouth of French Creek and decided to make his headquarters at the mouth of Turtle Creek. In addition, Frazier's settlement did gun making and repair. Frazier's settlement was an unusual combination of crafts and trades. The establishment of a blacksmith's shop made the future site of Braddock the first iron-working site in western Pennsylvania. This was the very beginning of Braddock's metalworking history, which remains active to this present day. John Frazier was a Scot, who had established an extensive trading network reaching as far as Michigan and Kentucky. Frazier's network was made up of Scots, Irish and English frontiersmen. Frazier was believed to be part Irish and was the start of a long history of the city of Braddock and the Irish. Frazier was the first "boy" of Braddock, who would touch the history of our nation. What is often overlooked is that young Frazier was part of a small group that established the first fort (Fort Prince George) at the present location of Pittsburgh. It can be claimed that it was a Braddock boy who founded Pittsburgh!

The other distinguished settler visited by George Washington in 1753 was the Seneca Chief, Queen Aliquippa. Queen Aliquippa was one of the oldest Indian diplomats in the region. Queen Aliquippa was known to have met with William Penn in 1701 as a representative of the Six Nations. Actually Queen Aliquippa's camp was upriver from Braddock's Field at merge of the Youghiogheny and the Monongahela. This particular delta historically was a corn farming area for the Indians. The Monongahela valley was also a source of rye used by Scots-Irish traders to make "Monongahela rye whiskey." Monongahela rye was really the grandfather of frontier whiskeys, which are today immortalized in Kentucky bourbon and Tennessee mash. Monongahela rye whiskey was prized throughout the colonies. It was shipped on the river networks to St. Louis and New Orleans. Drinking whiskey is the oldest continuous activity of the "Mon" valley. There were also horse caravans of Monongahela rye whiskey to the east. Monongahela whiskey rye was the real industry by the time of the Revolution; much larger than the fur trade so cherished by the French.

Whiskey, ginseng and furs were part of the major trade traffic to the east, while salt and iron moved back from the east to the Monongahela valley. By 1800 Monongahela grain flour grown on the river flood plains had become world famous: "is celebrated in foreign markets, for its superiority, and it generally sells for a dollar more per barrel in New Orleans than any other flour from this country."[7] Packhorses were the initial transportation but in the 1750s wagons came into use. In particular the Conestoga wagon moved trans-Allegheny freight. German wagon makers in the Conestoga Valley of Lancaster County invented the Conestoga wagon. These wagons also pushed the development of good roads from the Monongahela valley east. Indian paths such as the Raystown path became the basis for future Route 30 and the Pennsylvania Turnpike. These trade roads were again building a base for the industrial future of the Monongahela valley.

Monongahela rye whiskey, Monongahela flour and coal would dramatically increase the barge transportation industry in the area. Braddock, with its hardwoods, had barrel making and some boat making industries in the 1820s to 1840s. This transportation industry was another key to the future of steelmaking in the Monongahela valley. Pittsburgh grew in its shipbuilding industry as well because of the demand for Monongahela products. The famous riverboat used by the Lewis and Clark Expedition was built in Pittsburgh.

---

[7] Lamb, 35

Washington's few notes on his visits to the future Braddock suggested a very swift but shallow Monongahela. We know that he called it impassable by raft and switched to a canoe. There appeared to have also been rapids caused by a drop in water level. The canoe is particularly designed for this type of waters. The lower water level made the area strategically important to future armies to ford the river. Today Braddock is an important lock and dam location. George Washington noted he felt the "point" (Pittsburgh) was strategically the best location for a fort and settlement. The French disagreed that this point at present Pittsburgh was of strategic importance but targeted it because the British valued the site. The French and Irish traders favored sites like future Braddock, McKeesport and Logstown (Ambridge).

It should be noted that the main political center for the Indians of western Pennsylvania was neither Braddock's Field nor the future Pittsburgh but Logstown (present day Ambridge) on the Ohio River. Still the settlement of Frazier on the Monongahela was a major threat to the French empire in America. Frazier's associates could be found in the area of present day West Virginia, Kentucky, Ohio and the Great Lakes forming one of the largest American trade networks of the time. Most of the British traders, such as Frazier, worked in corporations, in contrast to the individual French traders whose trade was controlled by the French provincial government. The French had already thrown Frazier out of the northern part of Pennsylvania at Venango because of his threat to French commerce. Frazier's settlement at Turtle Creek was considered another real threat to the French. Frazier's trading post was a key rest stop on the road from Virginia. It was also a vital link in supply goods for English migration west. The partially built Fort Prince George at future Pittsburgh was a result of Washington's belief in the critical nature of the meeting of the Allegheny and Monongahela to form the Ohio

River. Neither the Indians nor the French considered this Pittsburgh delta strategically critical. In fact there is no sign of early Indian habitation of the Pittsburgh point site, probably because of the swampy nature of the "point" and spring flooding which remains a problem even to this day. Frazier's settlement and trading post was strategic for supplies, repairs and rest to the flow of English migration. The French saw Frazier's settlement as the real strategic center of the British occupation of the Monongahela valley.

Frazier's settlement did not have a formal deed. Frazier did live with his wife Nelly at the site until they died. The Frazier family remained in the area until the early 1800s. However the area directly across river was deeded in 1749 to notable Irish trader, George Croghan. This is actually the first known deed of land in the area. This Deed No. 1 referred to a piece of land "on the south side of the Monongahela River beginning at a run nearly opposite to Turtle Creek and down the Monongahela to its junction with the Ohio, computed to be ten miles." Croghan was a Dublin Irishman considered an "idol among his country men." It was estimated in 1750 that Croghan controlled over a fourth of all the Monongahela valley trade. While both Croghan and Frazier dealt in furs as well as trade, their settlements were trading posts and east-west distribution centers, since hunting was banned on the Monongahela under the terms of the 1750 Logstown treaty. These posts repaired guns, wagons and sold dry goods. They probably sold whiskey to the Indians as well. The flood plains were excellent gardens for corn and rye. Besides their own settlements, we know that both men were active in the building of Fort Prince George (named after future King George III) at present day Pittsburgh. Clearly the settlements of Frazier and Croghan would have threatened French ownership of the area and heightened the tensions.

Shortly after Washington's return to Williamsburg, Virginia, the uncompleted Fort Prince George fell to the French. A new major French fort was built and named Fort Duquesne after the French governor of the area. After the French occupation of Fort Duquesne, John Frazier's trading post was burned, and the area was claimed for New France. At Frazier's cabin the French raised their flag calling it Fort Machault. The name might have stuck if not for the upcoming great battle to be fought on that site.

George Washington returned to the area with a group of colonial militia, using his earlier route that would become Braddock's Road. This expeditionary force greatly improved the road as it moved into Monongahela country. Washington's expedition made it as far as Chestnut Ridge, fifty miles south of Pittsburgh. It was here that Washington's French encounter started what on this continent was known as the French and Indian War (the Seven Years War in Europe). It was a simple attack on a French scouting party under the command of Coulon de Jumonville. Jumonville died in the encounter in the wilderness that became known as the French and Indian War's equivalent to the Revolutionary War's "shot heard round the world." Upon news of Jumonville's death, Fort Duquesne sent a force of five hundred French and four hundred Canadian Indians by the Monongahela to Redstone and across the forest to Chestnut Ridge. Washington was surrounded and forced to surrender at the hastily built Fort Necessity in an area known as the Great Meadows.

The surrender at Fort Necessity was one of those "wake-up calls" that changed history. It caused a cry for uniting the colonies under British command. Benjamin Franklin was the leader of this new movement known as the Plan of Union. The British government assigned General Edward Braddock to command its military forces in North America. General Braddock was a seasoned soldier and Irish military commander. He was, however, schooled in traditional face-to-face warfare, which varied from the guerrilla tactics used in the woods of North America. In many ways, "Braddock's Defeat" would define the nature of fighting for American forces in future wars. It would be the tactical school for generals on both sides of the Revolutionary War.

Chapter Two

"Such was the complication of political interests, that a cannon shot fired in America could give the signal that set Europe ablaze."
—*Voltaire on Braddock's Defeat*

Braddock's Field

Braddock's Defeat would define the history of Britain, France and the United States. On the battlefield that day were a number of "boys" who would become future generals and statesmen who defined American history. It would require a major historical research effort to find any single battle that had so many significant future generals as Braddock's Defeat. To name a few there was George Washington; Thomas Gage, the future Revolutionary War commander of the British; and future Revolutionary War generals for the Americans, Horatio Gates, Charles Lee, Arthur St. Clair, John Neville, and Adam Stephen. Also present were Daniel Morgan, the famous riflemen commander, Daniel Boone, and the future war chief, Pontiac. Others included Indian scouts Christopher Gist and George Croghan. This young George Croghan would rise to colonel and play a key role in Ohio during the War of 1812. Another figure was colonial officer James Burd, the road-building engineer. Braddock's Defeat would augur the future defeat of the British in the Revolutionary War. This battle and the use of "guerrilla" tactics would change the way wars would be fought. Most importantly, the sword of an American victory would be forged from the steel of defeat. Washington had observed the secret to the defeat of the greatest army on the continent of Europe: the use of non-conventional tactics of guerilla warfare. It was to be the core of his future strategy in the Revolutionary War.

General Braddock arrived at Alexandria, Virginia in 1754. Edward Braddock was a graying, heavyset Irishman of sixty. Braddock had spent forty years working his way up the ranks in the Coldstream Guards. He was a proud officer who thought little of the colonials, Indians and the French. He seemed to have little respect for the young colonial commander, George Washington. Starting at Alexandria with British regulars and the colonial regiments of George Washington, Braddock cut a wilderness road following Washington's earlier expeditions. In total, General Braddock had 1400 regulars, 700 provincials, 50 sailors and a few Indians. Washington struggled for respect under Braddock's command but remained loyal. Washington's early routes to the Monongahela were followed and improved into a road. As they approached Frazier's cabin, they forded the river prior to the Turtle Creek gorge to avoid attack from the highlands. The army then crossed the Monongahela again to Frazier's cabin (present location of Edgar Thomson Works blast furnaces). General Braddock was surprised to have reached Frazier's clearing without attack. The British confidence soared with this success.

The opposing French at Fort Duquesne dispatched Captain Daniel Beaujeu with 250 French soldiers and sailors and 600 Indians. The French Indians were Canadian and western tribes (Miamis, Wyandots and others) as well as the local Delaware and Shawnee, who broke with the ruling Seneca. In addition the French won over a group of local bastard Iroquois (outcasts because of mixed marriages), the Mingos. The known presence of the future chief, Pontiac, suggests some Ottawas, Chippewas and Potawatomies and other Great Lakes Indian tribes were also at the battle.

On July 9, 1755, General Braddock had breakfast ahead of the main body on the future site of the town of Braddock. The

French troops were hearing morning mass at the first church in the area, The Assumption of Our Lady. The French feared defeat, and underestimated their Indian allies. Beaujeu was said to have lain at the altar asking for his troops to be spared. General Braddock had no idea that he would meet the French that day. He expected the battle to be a siege of Fort Duquesne, ten miles downriver.

The path had varied from Washington's earlier travels in that the army stalled at the deep gorge of Turtle Creek, choosing to ford the Monongahela and then ford back on the future site of Braddock's Field. The steep banks slowed their progress and made it difficult to move the artillery. It is known the there was a low but steep shore embankment that slowed artillery and heavy equipment. Well-hidden Indians and advanced French troops were in the hills overlooking the site. The advance British party was led by Lieutenant-Colonel Thomas Gage. The line of troops passed through the present junction of Jones and Bell avenues. It is believed that Gage in his haste failed to get the necessary intelligence. The French had artillery in the present location of Braddock Cemetery in North Braddock. I have often looked down from the French position near the cemetery and it is the perfect observation point. The French had a clear view of Braddock's movements throughout the battle.

The French fired first but the British fired back and panicked the younger and inexperienced French Canadians. After rallying, the French broke Gates's advance. The French then blended in and out of the forest, confusing the British commanders. Indian veterans later recalled that they had targeted George Washington but gave up saying, "fire at him no more; see ye not that the Great Spirit protects that chief; he cannot die in battle." Washington had his horse shot from under him and continued the fight.

Washington's heroism is a matter of legend. The American colonials in general distinguished themselves even in defeat. The British regulars were; however, soundly beaten. The British continued to fight in uniform open formations, while Washington argued with Braddock to fight like the French, using cover. One observer, colonial colonel James Burd reported: "General Braddock denied the request, and raged and stormed with vehemence, calling them cowards and dastards. He even went so far as to strike them with his drawn sword for attempting to adopt this mode of warfare."[1] What is lost in the shroud of the defeat; however, is the heroism of General Braddock. During the battle, Braddock was active in the line, having five horses shot from under him! He personally tried to rally the troops to recover Gates's artillery at the front of the line.

Braddock, of course, finally received a mortal wound and was carried from the battlefield, only to die four days later. One of the most interesting local traditions is that Braddock was shot by his "own" men. Several newspapers and local writers referred to a Uniontown man who actually claimed credit for it.[2] While recent historians have overlooked this local belief, it would seem possible, given the continuing arguments about the battle tactics before and during the fight. This, coupled with Braddock's actions against the colonials (using his sword) and his dislike of the colonials trying to change tactics, suggests at least the possibility. Braddock was heroic but he was also a hardheaded Irishman trying to lead hardheaded colonial Scots-Irish soldiers. Yet supposedly, Braddock's last words were: "We'll know what to do next time." The statement may have been revisionist colonial

---

[1] Daniel Rupp, *Early History of Western Pennsylvania, and of the West, and of western Expeditions* (Pittsburgh: D. W. Kaufman, 1846), 105
[2] ibid., 105

history but in any case the message was lost on his fellow British officers.

The battle caused a state of confusion in the British lines. Many accounts go much further, calling it panic. Braddock seemed to remain in control in the face of the confusion until being brought down by a bullet. General Braddock freed the main body and allowed for men to defend the artillery running north from today's Edgar Thomson blast furnaces to Center Avenue. The panic appeared rooted in the hearts of the soldiers who feared the Indians: "the men from what storys they had heard of the Indians, in reguard to their scalping; and mohawking, were so panick Struck, that their officers had little or no Command over them."[3] The British finally totally broke down and ran from the field of battle. Washington managed to regroup the army across river on top of Kennywood hill. There the army paused to drink from a spring known as Braddock's Spring, which is located at the present day amusement ride, the Jack Rabbit, in Kennywood Park. It is now clear that Braddock, despite his bravery, managed the engagement poorly. Braddock's doctors are believed to have said he died as much from depression as his wounds. The defeat by the French and Indians was a humiliation and had he lived, probably would have ended his career.

Ultimately the day was a great defeat for the British. *The battle remains the bloodiest defeat Britain had ever suffered on the North American continent.* In George Washington's own words: "The shocking scenes which presented themselves in this nights March are not to be described. The dead, the dying, the groans, lamentation, and cries along the road of the wounded for help ... were enough to pierce a heart of adamant."[4] Braddock's army suffered 456 dead and 421

---

[3] Paul Kopperman, *Braddock at the Monongahela* (Pittsburgh: University of Pittsburgh Press, 1977), 72
[4] ibid., 91

wounded. Of the 83 commissioned British officers, 63 were killed or wounded. Two of the British officers from the Scottish Dragoons killed that day were distant relatives of Andrew Carnegie, a man who would be the builder of the town of Braddock in the 1800s. There are reports of many wounded and scalped soldiers who dragged themselves into the forest to die. This may account for the existence of British artifacts still being found in neighboring boroughs such as Swissvale. The retreat was disorderly with much of the artillery left on the field or stuck in the river during the re-crossing of the Monongahela. Braddock died four days later and had to be buried unmarked in the trail to avoid mutation by the Indians. In 1804, some men working on the building of the National Road found human remains around the spot where Braddock was reportedly buried. The remains were re-buried in a grassy knoll nearby with a marker finally being added in 1913. Washington is given much credit for at least saving what was left of the beaten army. Wagoner Daniel Boone is also noted for his role in the retreat and burial of Braddock. Tradition has it that the handful of British Indian allies under Queen Aliquippa escaped via an old Indian trail (now Swissvale Avenue) from Wilkinsburg to Kittanning, on the night of the defeat.[5]

The night of the defeat also brought much celebration at Fort Duquesne (Pittsburgh). This included the proud display of bloody scalps and body parts. The Indians brought in prisoners and tortured them. The French reports are scandalous: "the Indians even resorted to cannibalism on that dreadful day, drinking broth made from the flesh of their victims. There were scalps, hundreds of blond, brown, or black British scalps, still dripping blood as the savages stretched them on hoops to

---

[5] Mary Davison, editor, *Annals of Old Wilkinsburg and Vicinity*, (Wilkinsburg: The Group, 1940), 29

cure."[6] The celebrations went on for days using captured British rum.

The battlefield was left as is, except for the French and Indian dead, which were taken to Fort Duquesne for burial. The British left under hot pursuit and their dead remained on the field. Reports are that hordes of bears came to feast on the flesh. Legends lasted for decades that man-eating bears haunted Braddock's Field for years after because of their cravings for human flesh. Five years later a visiting British officer reported: "We saw many men's bones along the shore. We kept along the road about 1-1/2 miles, where the first engagement begun, where there are men's bones lying about as thick as leaves do on ground; for they are so thick that one lies on top of another for about a half a mile in length, and about hundred yards in breadth."[7] Even after fifty-six years, a traveler noted: "we traveled about a mile, when we came to the ground where Gen. Braddock was defeated. Many memorials of the battle are still to be seen, but none so characteristic as the bones which lay bleaching by the wayside."[8] In 1883 when the Lake Erie Railroad started digging to lay tracks, a number of skeletons were turned up. Even today, when construction digging takes place many artifacts from the battle will be found. My grandfather told me of hundreds of artifacts and bones being found in the building of St. Thomas Catholic Church in the early 1900s (St. Thomas was destroyed by fire in the 1980's).

It is truly a loss that such a great battlefield was not made a national park. Today a great deal of that battlefield is under the Edgar Thomson Works of United States Steel Corporation.

---

[6] Leland Baldwin, *Pittsburgh–The Story of a City*, 41
[7] Kopperman, 92
[8] Rupp, 137

While Washington, Gates and other colonial officers grew from the defeat, the British missed the opportunity. Thomas Gage would be the future British commander of the American continent and opposed Washington in the Revolutionary War. Gage seemed to have missed the message of the failure of regular military techniques and put the blame on the "scandalous behavior" of the men. He also felt that the failure of the colonials to fight to support such tactics led to failure.[9] The defeat caused an uproar in Europe. The British Parliament required an investigation of the defeat. Gage and the British officers held to their stand that the colonials' failure to fight European-style was the problem. A few officers off the record did admit the French and Indian tactics were superior. Gage and Washington would replay the strategies over and over during the upcoming Revolutionary War.

The French occupation of the Monongahela lasted only to November of 1758. In the summer of 1758 a massive force of British and colonials was assembled in the states of Maryland, Pennsylvania and Virginia. The force of over 6,000 men was under the command of Scottish General John Forbes. His right-hand man was a Swiss colonel, Henry Bouquet, who had studied and learned from Braddock's Defeat. In addition, Braddock veterans St. Clair, Washington, Burd and others were part of the force. This expedition came by way of the Raystown path, not Braddock's Road. The French were watching Braddock's Road, as it was the choice of officers such as Washington.[10] A lead party under Major James Grant, trying for personal fame, attacked Fort Duquesne days ahead of the main body but was beaten on September 4. Forbes was, however, a very deliberate campaigner, building forts and covering his rear.

---

[9] Kopperman, 190-192
[10] Buck and Buck, 94

The final part of Forbes's campaign was launched from Fort Ligonier on November 17. On the night of the November 24, the army camped near Braddock's Field at Turtle Creek. This time the French at Fort Duquesne realized the situation was hopeless. They burned the fort and moved north. On November 27, 1758, the fort was christened Fort Pitt. Fort Pitt held the area for the British during Pontiac's War of 1763. Pontiac's uprising did pull the Monongahela settlers to Fort Pitt for protection, vacating most of the Monongahela valley.

The years prior to the Revolution saw a slow influx of Irish and Scottish settlers. Braddock's Field remained only as a part of the path to Fort Pitt. The Indians did, however, continue to plant corn at Braddock. The revolutionary years passed with few events of note. Further up river in 1768, the Irishman, David McKee, established a homestead at the present site of McKeesport. Post-Revolution, Braddock's Field at times was used for military training. After the Revolution there was an influx of ex-Tories and pacifists into the Monongahela valley.[11] At the same time there was also an exodus to the new frontier in Kentucky. The racial mix of the Monongahela valley remained the same with the exception of a slight increase of English.

Braddock's Field, as it was known in the 1700s, was again to bust onto the national scene in 1794 during the Whiskey Rebellion. As noted, the major cash product of the Monongahela valley was rye whiskey. A federal excise tax placed on it in 1792 caused a new stirring in the valley. The excise tax was 7 cents on the gallon, which was a 25% tax! The Irish and Scottish settlers were particularly sensitive to this type of tax since excise taxes in Ireland and Scotland were a sign of oppression.

Rye grew abundantly in the Monongahela valley. This rye as noted was of extremely high quality but it had to be sold in

---

[11] Baldwin, 97

the east. Lightweight products such as rye grain were very expensive to move by wagon or packhorses to the east. Shipping by river to New Orleans and then by ship to New York could be competitive at times with wagon trains over the eastern mountains. Around 1800, a bushel of rye sold for 40 cents in the east. Whiskey, which required a bushel and half to make a gallon of whiskey, then sold for over a dollar a gallon in New York. In effect that meant you got forty cents more per bushel of rye by using it to make whiskey. The shipping costs of higher density whiskey were much lower as well. One analysis in about 1794 showed: "as a packhorse carried two eight gallon gourds, the shipment on the back of a single horse brought $16, or ten times more than one received for the four bushels that the packhorse carried before."[12]

In the 1790s, the new federal government imposed a tax on frontier whiskey. A group in the Monongahela valley formed to take up arms if necessary against the collectors of this whiskey tax. One of that group, George Wallace, owned Braddock's Field.[13] The group called for a military muster at Braddock's Field. Braddock's Field was to become a symbol of resistance against centralized government. The "Pittsburgh militia" was led by Henry Brackenridge and General John Wilkins. The muster was a "show" of force against the federal government. Mainly it was a drunken party. Still "some pieces of artillery lost on the retreat of Braddock in the channel of the river" were drawn out and prepared.[14] Leaders called for a burning of Pittsburgh, the seat of federal authority. The "army" of 5000 marched from Braddock's Field down

---

[12] Stefan Lorant, *Pittsburgh: The Story of an American City* (Lenox, Massachusetts: Authors Edition Inc., 1964), 57
[13] Leland D. Baldwin, *Whiskey Rebels* (Pittsburgh: University of Pittsburgh Press, 1939), 146
[14] ibid., 157

Braddock Avenue and through Pittsburgh and Washington County as a demonstration.

The then President George Washington assembled an army. This assembled federal army came using Braddock's Road and was headed by Washington himself as far as Cumberland, Maryland. This army marched on Braddock's Field and Pittsburgh in 1794 to put down the rebellion. While the Braddock muster ended in several days, the federal army did make an appearance in the Monongahela valley but there was no fighting. Ultimately the Whiskey Rebellion found a political solution. The whiskey and brewing industry did move west to Kentucky where the tax could be avoided for a few more years. This settlement of the Whiskey Rebellion allowed for the continued prosperity in transportation and trade in the Monongahela valley. The political radicalism survived in the formation of the Democratic-Republican Party in opposition to the Federalist Party. The Monongahela valley gave strong support to Thomas Jefferson as a result.

The decade after the War of 1812 saw a decline in prosperity due to the National Road going through Wheeling rather than Pittsburgh. Still the Monongahela valley had strong riverboat traffic but some frontier products such as whiskey were being lost to the new frontier. At the same time demand for Monongahela coal and sand for glass making was increasing. In 1797, the first glass was blown in Pittsburgh. The glass was "green" because of the poor quality of the sand. In 1803, using Monongahela sand, Pittsburgh became a producer of high flint glass. By 1820, this flint glass was heralded as: "superior to that made in the East and was in demand all over the country."[15] In addition to glass, Monongahela pottery was also popular in the midwestern frontier. Thanks to the natural blessing of coal, the Monongahela valley became the glass valley of the world. As

---

[15] Leland Baldwin, *Pittsburgh–The Story of a City*, 149

with its prior history, the Monongahela valley success was a combination of the river, natural resources, and high quality products and providence.

A major event for Braddock's Field in this time period was a visit in 1825 by the Marquis De Lafayette (Washington's young French general in the Revolutionary War). Lafayette visited the Wallace farm and mansion. George Wallace had built a farm on the old battlefield. Wallace was also a veteran of the Revolutionary War. Lafayette had come to the field of one of France's greatest military victories in North America, but just as important, it was the field that forged the career of his old friend, George Washington. Lafayette pored over the details of the battle throughout the visit. Historian John Boucher recorded the following: "in this Lafayette and his party were entertained, and they spent considerable time in going over the battlefield, discussing the unfortunate defeat. Though seventy years had passed since the battle, the farmer could scarcely draw a furrow without turning up bones whitened by time and fragments of arms corroded by rust."[16] Another note of significant history connected to George Wallace was his slave, Mrs. Barkley or "Black Bab" who was the first black resident of Braddock. At the time of Lafayette's visit, Braddock's Field was still wooded with a few farms. Other than some river traffic, there was no commercial activity at Braddock's Field. Pittsburgh on the other hand became a city in 1816. Braddock's now vanished neighbor, Port Perry, was starting to develop into a town from the river traffic.

From 1795 to the Civil War, Braddock's Field developed into a small village of little significance. Actually Port Perry, now a railroad junction at the end of Braddock was a larger town.

---

[16] John Newton, *A Century and a half of Pittsburg and Her People* (Pittsburgh: Lewis Publishing Company, 1908), 405

Monongahela River transportation was, however, a growth industry. The now ghost town of Port Perry at the Braddock city boundary was popular as a stopping point for river men. Transportation on the Monongahela was limited to high water times until 1840 when the Number Seven dam and Number Eleven lock system was set up. This system allowed the Monongahela to be navigable as far as Brownville. The motivation for river development was the huge demand for Monongahela coal and pig iron by the foundries of Pittsburgh. Port Perry/Braddock became a key river lock/dam at the location that George Washington noted as impassable in low water. Port Perry had a number of repair shops as well such as a blacksmith shop and a cooper shop for barrels. In 1850, the Pennsylvania Railroad was extended through Braddock to Port Perry where passengers could get a stagecoach for twenty-eight miles and connect with railroads east. When the first train came from Port Perry to Pittsburgh in 1852, the crowd at Pittsburgh included Andrew Carnegie, Edgar Thomson and famous songwriter, Stephen Foster (a Pittsburgher). Stephen Foster's brother William was the engineer of the first train. While Braddock remained a farm field, Port Perry got a US Post Office in 1850. Braddock did have a small barrel factory in 1850.

Turtle Creek was also flourishing as a town many years prior to Braddock. Turtle Creek had grown in the late 1700s as a stagecoach stop. During one of Washington's several visits to Turtle Creek, he noted in his journal of dining at the "widow's Dower's." By 1790 the Widow Meyer's Hotel or Tavern, where Washington stopped had become a popular stagecoach stop. Port Perry and Turtle Creek appeared to have a bright future compared to the sleepy village of Braddock.

The town of Braddock did, however, have some important attributes. First it was at a lock and dam, which made it a stopping point for river travel. It had two of the nation's major railroads crossing through as well. It was becoming a major railroad stop to load up the coal mined in the hills of Braddock and transport it to the foundries of Pittsburgh. Businessmen such as Thomas Dickson and James Corey were becoming wealthy partners of Pittsburgh's Judge Mellon, building a coal business. Braddock Avenue (the old military road) was one of the main county roads and connected to major roads east. The rye whiskey production, while declining, was still a key industry until the 1830s.

Chapter 3

"The Carnegie Steel Company, as will be seen from this narrative, is not the creation of any man, nor indeed of any set of men."
—*James Bridge, 1903*

Iron Comes to the Valley

When John Frazier set up his blacksmith shop in 1742, there was no iron being produced in the Monongahela valley. Furs and rye whiskey were used for barter to bring in iron from the east. The British government restricted area development in iron production with special taxes that slowed the early growth of iron making in the colonies. Even William Pitt, from whom Pittsburgh derives its name, opposed any colonial iron industry capable of competing with the British iron industry. Pitt is believed to have said in Parliament: "I am opposed to allowing the colonists to make even a hob-nail for themselves." The first iron furnace in America was at Falling Creek, near Richmond, Virginia in 1620. These colonial furnaces were known as charcoal furnaces since charcoal was the fuel used. Charcoal was produced from hardwood trees. Furnace location required a source of iron ore, limestone, acres of hardwoods, a hill for construction and furnace top loading, and finally a water source to power it. Besides waterpower and hills, the Monongahela valley had the best hardwood for iron making: hickory and black oak. The simple fact is that the "Iron" city and valley lacks one key ingredient for iron making: iron ore! It did have a secret ingredient, that of rye whiskey. One furnace historian noted: "hard liquor was in great demand by the workmen. It was almost as necessary as food or so it seemed."[1]

Whiskey and hardwood would not be enough to transform the Monongahela valley into the iron center of the world. The key event, however, would be the merger of nearby Connellsville coal and the great iron furnaces of Carnegie that would form the Steel Valley of the Pittsburgh and Braddock area. That achievement would come from a Braddock boy who lived almost on the old site of Frazier's trading post in the 1840s.

Officially the first iron furnace west of the Alleghenies was Alliance Furnace. (Unofficial research of my own suggests the title belongs to Peter Tar's Furnace at present day Weirton, West Virginia.) In any case, Alliance Furnace was at the headwaters of the Youghiogheny River and started operation around 1789. Alliance Furnace cast cannonballs and other armaments. It was known to have supplied Mad Anthony Wayne's troops prior to marching out of base camp at Logstown (Ambridge) in the late 1700s. Alliance Furnace operated only a few years, probably because of the low-grade iron ore.

The product of a charcoal iron furnace was "pig" iron. These pigs were made by running molten (liquid) iron into dirt trenches on the furnace floor. There was a main runner coming from the tap hole of the furnace. Then side runners were made in a treelike structure. Because the side runners looked like baby suckling pigs feeding off a mother pig, the term pig iron came into common usage. The pig is a rectangular block running 12 to 24 inches long and 6 inches by 2 inches on the end. The liquid pig iron was a product of charcoal taking away the oxygen in iron ore (known as smelting or reducing) to

---

[1] Myron Sharp and William Thomas, *A Guide to the Old Stone Blast Furnaces in Western Pennsylvania* (Pittsburgh: The Historical Society of Western Pennsylvania, 1966), 3

produce iron. This iron, however, is not pure elemental iron but a mixture of carbon and iron. The "pigs" weighed about 10 to 100 pounds to allow easy handling. Pig iron is an intermediate product that was then sold to foundries to re-melt and make shaped products. Some of the charcoal furnaces directly cast products such as stoves, skillets, Dutch ovens, etc. To the non-metallurgist, the terms pig iron and cast iron are confusing. *Chemically, pig and cast iron can be considered the same. Pig iron refers to block-like shapes, while the term "cast iron" refers to shapes that are formed to produce an object such as an oven. While we are at it, blast-furnace iron is also chemically the same, but designates the molten metal.*

George Anshutz built the first iron furnace in Pittsburgh in 1793. The furnace ran less than two years because of the shortage of local ore and the expense of shipping in ore. It wasn't until 1859 that another furnace was built in Allegheny County. The location was the south side of Pittsburgh on Carson Street below Mount Washington. While the operation failed it did utilize the new coke technology instead of wood charcoal. Prior to 1840, all pig iron produced in the country was made from charcoal. From 1840 coal/coke furnaces started to increase dramatically. The use of coke from coal was to make the Monongahela valley the future steel valley. By 1860 only 30% of the pig iron in the United States was from charcoal, the balance being coal/coke mixes. In 1884 charcoal furnace production of pig iron had dropped to under 10%.[2]

While coal was the primary source of fuel for iron making in England, it wasn't until 1840 that its use started in America. Charcoal actually is a superior fuel for iron making because it lacks impurities such as sulfur. Its major shortcoming is that it

---

[2] Peter Temin, *Iron and Steel in Nineteenth Century America* (Cambridge, Massachusetts: M.I.T Press, 1964), Appendix c.3

required an acre of hardwood to run a furnace for one day. Even the great forests of the Monongahela valley could not have supplied the industry but a few decades. In fact northern Michigan, which was rich in iron ore but lacked coal, did start charcoal iron making in 1860 but lumbered out the area in less than two decades. It is said of charcoal furnaces that: "each week the small ironworks consumed a football field of virgin forest to produce a few tons of pig iron."[3] The charcoal iron furnace has long since disappeared in the United States, but today the Brazilian iron making industry is using charcoal as fuel and is the major reason for the loss of the rain forests.

Still the industry was slow to switch over to coal, which did not account for 90% of production until the 1880s. As late as World War One in the United States, charcoal furnaces were brought back in service to supply the demands of war. Charcoal inherently limited the amount of pig iron that could be produced out of the furnace. The low physical strength of charcoal would not have supported the high blast furnaces of the future Edgar Thomson Works.

While iron smelting was seeing slow growth in the Monongahela valley, the iron foundry business based on the re-melting of shipped iron bars was growing rapidly as the Civil War approached. The foundry business primarily required good sources of fuel. Pittsburgh had two excellent sources of fuel-natural gas and coal. Charcoal pig iron could be shipped down the Monongahela from the furnaces in the mountains east of Pittsburgh. Actually the foundry business was well under way in the early 1800s. In 1805, a group of Pittsburgh investors started an iron foundry to re-melt iron pig bars. These iron bars were coming from areas up the Monongahela valley such as Cambria County near present day Johnstown. This Pittsburgh foundry was a key supplier of

---

[3] John Stubbles, *The Original Steel Makers* (Warrendale: Iron and Steel Society, 1984), 7

Iron Comes to the Valley

cannons, cannonballs and shells to Commodore Perry in 1812. Like the glass industry it was being driven by the abundance of high quality coal in the Monongahela valley. It was why financiers such as Thomas Mellon were investing in the Braddock coalmines prior to the Civil War. Coal, besides being cheap, did offer another very important technical advantage. The advantage was a high heating output but it came at a high price to the environment in the form of heavy, sulfur-smelling air pollution. It was in 1830 that Charles Dickens on a visit to Pittsburgh noted: "Pittsburgh is like Birmingham in England, at least its towns people say so.... It certainly has a quantity of smoke hanging over it, and is famous for its iron works.

By the 1850s, Pittsburgh was supplying the iron castings for the great Industrial Revolution. The first industry of Braddock was the McKay-Walker Foundry, which made small arms supplies for the federal government during the Civil War. The McKay-Walker foundry used the abundant local coal for a heating fuel. Later this first Braddock foundry would be critical to the construction of Edgar Thomson Works in 1875. In 1854 Pittsburgh had 38 foundries in operation. One fourth of these foundries were producing cast iron for steam engines exclusively.[4]

The major use of pig iron from 1835 to 1860 was the production of wrought iron railroad rails. Wrought iron is made by heating cast pig iron to white hot and working it by forging, rolling or puddling. Machinery parts tended to be forged. Rails were made by puddling, forging, rolling or combinations of these processes. Further discussion requires a little metallurgy.

Cast, pig or blast-furnace iron is produced when carbon (from charcoal, coal or coke) is used to reduce iron from its

---

[4] Peter Temin, *Pennsylvania Notes* (Pittsburgh: University of Pittsburgh, 1940), 38

oxide ore. Simply put, the carbon combines with oxygen in the iron ore forming gaseous carbon dioxide and high carbon iron. The resulting cast iron or pig iron is very high in carbon content (around 3%). Cast iron physically is very brittle and can be broken with a hammer. It is the carbon in the iron that makes it brittle. Cast iron has its uses: it flows in liquid form out of the charcoal or blast furnace. This allows it to be cast in detailed shapes such as stoves and complex machine parts. Automotive engine blocks are still today produced from cast iron. Besides its brittle nature it has some other unique characteristics. First, it has excellent heat transfer properties. Cast iron hearth plates were used in colonial fireplaces to radiate more heat into the room. These properties led Benjamin Franklin to use it to make stoves. It also absorbs sound and vibrations, making it excellent for large machinery bases. When it came to rails, cast iron was originally used for small early locomotives. As the weight of locomotives and cargo increased by 1845, cast iron was too brittle for most applications.

Wrought iron, on the other hand, is soft, workable and malleable. The reason for this workability was due to the removal of carbon. Removing carbon from pig iron produces wrought iron. One way to remove carbon is to heat the pig iron up and "work" it in some way. For centuries, blacksmith and sword smiths have used this technique using only heat, a hammer and anvil to produce small amounts of wrought iron and steel. In colonial times large amounts could be produced using a "refinery" forge or "bloom." The treatment of "heat and beat" produces wrought iron with a very low carbon content (less than .2% carbon). A little less heating and beating can produce steel, which is between .2% and 1% carbon. As you remove carbon the product becomes more flexible and ductile. Wrought iron makes excellent rail material because it can absorb the pounding of heavy, fast moving trains. It has what metallurgists call high impact strength, while cast iron has low impact strength. Its main drawback is that wrought iron wears much faster than cast iron under load.

An Englishman, Henry Cort, invented puddling in 1784. Puddling uses very high heat, bringing the iron to a liquid. This pasty mass can easily be worked by a "puddler" into wrought iron. Heating and using a mechanical rolling mill can produce similar results. Puddling was best described as: "reduced to liquid form and boiled and stirred about until most of the impurities were driven off. When the bubbling mass thickened and assumed a pasty consistency, the puddler passed a long bar through a small opening in the furnace door, and rolled the paste into a ball." The pasty ball was crushed and rolled over and over by the puddler. "The ball was then reheated, and passed under hammers and through rollers; and the kneading it thus repeatedly underwent gave it the fibrous quality of wrought iron."[5] Some rolling mills used a form of puddling prior to rolling. Puddling was extremely popular in the new iron works of Wheeling, West Virginia, which were major nail producers.

One of the first puddling, rolling mills in Pittsburgh was the firm of Jones, Lauth, and Company in1853. The puddlers of Pittsburgh formed the first ironworkers "union" in 1858, the Sons of Vulcan. The Sons was a secret lodge organization using secret signs and passwords. The local lodge was called a "forge" and the president, the "Grand Vulcan." The membership of this specialized organization was limited to Irish, German, Welsh or Scots. Other, more recent immigrants, such as those from southern Europe, were not allowed into these "Vulcan" lodges. The Sons of Vulcan used a fraternity system to restrict membership to puddlers and higher paying

---

[5] James Bridge, *The Inside History of the Carnegie Steel Company*. (New York, New York: Aldine Book Company, 1903), 142

jobs. The Sons favored the Irish. Rollers who tended to be Welsh formed a different union.

Some rolling mills used a reversing technique, which moved the rail back and forth over the rolls. This reversing keeps working the iron and "refining" it. Reversing mills were first used in Britain. Another type of rail mill was pioneered by the Johnstown, Pennsylvania, company, Cambria Iron Works. Besides this Johnstown rolling mill, most rolling mills were in the eastern United States closer to the railroad center. There was a major rolling mill in Detroit supplying the west. Up until 1852, most rails were being imported from England because of higher quality and lower price. In 1852 technology and prices allowed the Americans to break into this huge iron market. By 1870, Allegheny County had thirty-three rolling mills producing an array of products including rails.

Other uses for pig/cast iron were the production of water and sewer pipes. Philadelphia was the first city to use cast iron pipes in 1820. The first cast pipe foundry west of the Alleghenies was Etna Iron Works of Pittsburgh, established in 1828. Cast iron building fronts were being used in cities like St. Louis and Pittsburgh as early as 1850. Eight cast iron front buildings were put up in Pittsburgh between 1840 and 1870. Some of these can still be seen today.

During the Civil War, the Fort Pitt Cannon Foundry became the leading producer of Union ordnance. It only had one rival in quality and production, that being the Tredegar Works of the Confederacy. Fort Pitt Foundry's fame was worldwide when it cast the biggest gun in the world for the Union. Captain Thomas Rodman, U.S. Army Ordnance Corps, designed the gun. It was known as a 15-inch Columbiad. By the end of the Civil War, Fort Pitt Foundry had cast over 3000 cannons and ten million pounds of shot. Some of these guns manned the famous Union ironclad battleship, *Monitor*. In general, the Civil War brought great prosperity to the

IRON COMES TO THE VALLEY

Monongahela valley. This prosperity resulted in the real threat that the Confederacy's J. E. B. Stuart and his cavalry might attack the Monongahela valley in 1863. There are local legends that Confederate gunboats were on the Monongahela, as well as Confederate raids might occur in the valley. Some suggest that Jeb Stewart came close to attacking the valley prior to the battle of Gettysburg and this accounted for his lateness at the battle and ultimate defeat of the Confederacy.

The Pittsburgh iron foundries were out-producing most of the nation by 1870. The foundry business was simply to take cold pig iron and re-melt it, finally casting it into usable shapes such as stoves and machine parts. The iron foundries used air (coal fired) furnaces to re-melt pig iron bars. The most common re-melt furnace is a stack called a cupola. Iron pigs are charged in the stack with coal or coke as a fuel, which produces liquid cast iron. Smelting furnaces for pig iron production had not been successful in the Pittsburgh area because of the lack of high quality iron ore. Ore deposits in Lawrence, Fayette and Cambria counties east of the Monongahela valley were limited, but were good sources of iron ore to produce pig iron in charcoal furnaces. This Pennsylvania ore is a limonite and hematite in mixed veins. In addition these iron ore veins are located beside a ferriferous limestone, which was an outstanding flux for the iron making process. Still charcoal furnaces opened and ran but a few years in any locality until the iron ore deposit ran out and then the operation moved on. There were hundreds of these furnaces scattered throughout western Pennsylvania. Many of these furnace stacks are still standing. There is even an excellent guide published of the location of these many abandoned furnaces.[6]

The demand for pig iron and coal for Pittsburgh foundries was enormous. English pig iron could be shipped up the Ohio

---

[6] Sharp and Thomas

River from New Orleans, as well as by rail from Philadelphia. Major iron finds were made in the Missouri area in the 1850s. Missouri started charcoal iron production and shipped charcoal pig iron via the Mississippi and Ohio to Pittsburgh foundries. Even a limited amount of charcoal furnace pig iron was coming in from the Great Lakes iron districts.

Iron makers were realizing that the ideal would be to bring the iron ore to the Monongahela valley, which had coal. Coal could then be made into a new fuel: coke. It is always economically efficient to ship the heavier and denser ingredient. Coke was a more thermally efficient fuel and would be cheaper than charcoal. Its strength allowed for high blast furnace stack. A blast furnace by definition used coke as fuel. The use of coke allowed for much higher stacks and diameter furnaces, which in turn greatly increased pig iron production. Coke is made by heating coal in bee ovens for long periods. The coke technology would start a boom for Monongahela coal in the 1850s.

Cambria Iron Company of Johnstown, a company that would play a major role in the future of Braddock, was a pioneer in the use of high production coke blast furnaces. The genealogy of Cambria Iron goes back to a veteran of Braddock's Field, General Arthur St. Clair. St. Clair opened a charcoal furnace known as Hermitage Furnace in 1803 near Johnstown. In 1819 this operation was moved to Johnstown. In 1832, the furnaces became Cambria Iron Company. Finally in 1853 the charcoal furnaces became coke blast furnaces, which fueled the great rail rolling mill.

Coke also changed the nature of the coal industry in the Monongahela valley. While Braddock's "Pittsburgh seam" was used for coke making, it was better suited for heating as in the foundries. A softer vein of the Pittsburgh coal seam near Connellsville became the coal of choice for making coke. The Connellsville coal was cheaper to mine and of very low sulfur content. Low sulfur coke was a requirement of quality iron making.

To fully understand the history of iron and steel making requires some discussion of coal mineralogy. Coal comes in three basic forms: lignite, bituminous, and anthracite. Lignite is a low-grade version with no industrial application but it can be used, as in Ireland, to heat homes. Anthracite is the hardest and has the highest carbon and energy content. Anthracite is also low in impurities. Anthracite coal is a "natural" coke and to a limited degree was used as a fuel to replace charcoal directly in early smelting furnaces. One problem of anthracite is that supplies are very limited and it can be high in sulfur, which the coking process burns out. Bituminous coal is the most common. The Pennsylvania coalfields are mostly bituminous. From 1776 to 1950, 90 percent of all the pig iron manufactured in the United States was made from coke make from "Pittsburgh seam" coal. It was the industrial seam for the world! Still the reader may ask, why make coke? The main reason to make coke from coal is to remove two impurities, sulfur and phosphorus. Additionally, a side benefit is that coke has better loading strength allowing for bigger furnaces (higher furnace stacks).

Sulfur and phosphorus are the real bad boys of iron and steel chemistries. Sulfur and phosphorus in coal and/or coke is transferred to the pig iron produced. The ideal is to start with a low sulfur/phosphorus coal and coke it removing any more. A very small amount of these two elements in iron (and steel) cause a great deal of problems. In casting, high sulfur iron causes a problem known as hot tearing. Hot tearing splits castings around sharp corners. A very similar problem, called hot shortness, occurs when rolling or forging iron rails. Hot shortness causes rails to split open on rolling. Sulfur and phosphorus, besides causing these processing problems, produce an inferior final iron product. In this case the brittleness of iron (and steel) increases with the content of sulfur and phosphorus in the steel. Sulfur and phosphorus can also, for example, make railroad rails sensitive to cold weather breakage. The coking process burns coal in a "beehive" furnace to remove these impurities.

Coke was becoming the main product in the Connellsville area by 1870. It would be a Braddock boy that would tie together the coke works of Connellsville with the furnaces of Braddock. A young Henry Clay Frick was main owner of Connellsville coke. That Braddock boy, James Corey (Father of William Corey), would also forge the first ties of the Carnegie Empire with Mellon Bank as well as spark one of America's richest industrialists. If young Frick was to become a major supplier of coke to the emerging Carnegie Empire, he needed a loan of $10,000 dollars to open ten more coke ovens. He had applied to Mellon Bank, but the loan officer turned him down.[7] His fate would depend on a Braddock boy, James Corey. James Corey had become a coal expert working his father's Braddock mines. Maybe just as important, Corey was a partner with the major banking enterprise of Judge Mellon. Mellon sent Corey to look and make the decision on the Frick loan. Corey filed the following short report: "lands good, ovens well built; keeps books evenings, maybe a little too enthusiastic about pictures but not enough to hurt; knows his business down to the ground; advise making the loan."[8] That concise approval would launch the great career of Frick and one of the largest accumulations of wealth ever made.

In 1859, James Laughlin built the first blast furnaces in Pittsburgh on the north side the Monongahela River. These were the now famous Eliza furnaces. In addition, "beehive"

---

[7] Martha Frick Symington Sanger, *Henry Clay Frick* (New York: Abbeville Press, 1998), 44

[8] George Harvey, *Henry Clay Frick* (Pittsburgh: Charles Scribner's Sons, 1928), 42

coke ovens were built there to change coal into coke. Later that same year another firm built the Clinton Blast Furnace in Pittsburgh to produce pig iron for foundries, rolling mills and forges. Local pig iron served even more foundries in the area. Additionally, two blast furnaces were built in 1863 called Superior Furnaces. All of these furnaces were 45 feet high and had twelve-foot bottom diameters (called the bosh). But the talk of steel makers around the world was the Struthers furnace near Youngstown, Ohio. This monster was fifty-five feet high and had a bottom diameter of sixteen feet. The Struthers furnace had a record production of 1600 tons in 1870.

The roots of the future Carnegie Steel can be found in 1858 on the present site of Midvale. This operation was the brainchild of two Prussian brothers, Anthony and Andrew Kloman. The Klomans forged iron railroad axles and wheels. Their location in Pittsburgh, like the foundries, was based on the abundance of Monongahela coal. The forge took the name Iron City Forge Company. Later this forge would become part of Carnegie Steel and the Kloman brothers would become partners with Carnegie.

Carnegie's great empire was built on an infrastructure of friendship. It has roots all the way back to his early childhood. It was an amazing network of boys that would ultimately control industrial America. The network started in the ghetto of Allegheny (north side of Pittsburgh) as a kid's gang, which they called the original six. Like all city kids they hung out together. The original six was made up of Andrew Carnegie, Thomas Miller, William Cowley, John Phipps (younger brother of Henry Phipps), James Smith, and James Wilson. Another younger related group tagged along. This group consisted of Tom Carnegie (Andrew's brother), Henry Phipps, and Henry W. Oliver, and Robert Pitcairn. The overall gang should have been called the league of extraordinary boys. The names read like a "Who's Who" of the iron and steel industry, as well as a street name map of western Pennsylvania. "The Gangs of Pittsburgh" could be a movie title about the Carnegie gang and its rival anti-Scottish gang of native Alleghenians called the "the bottom hoosiers."

The original six-plus-four would be the nucleus of Carnegie's future empire. Those boys did more than fight the native Alleghenians. The boys befriended a War of 1812 veteran, Colonel James Anderson. Colonel Anderson lived in the better part of Allegheny city. Anderson had a fifteen-hundred-volume library, which he made available to boys in the city of Allegheny. The group, in particular Andrew Carnegie, started to read and discuss. They were a lot like one of their heroes, Ben Franklin, a century earlier with his boys' group known as the Juno. The original six loved to discuss and dream about famous leaders: "they had discussed the campaigns of George Washington and the heroes of Sir Walter Scott."[9] Carnegie was greatly impacted by Colonel Anderson; later when Carnegie built a library in old Allegheny, he added a statute of Anderson in front of the building. As the boys grew they went to church together, were part of a singing group and loved to explore the river cliffs. This group would turn up again and again in the life of Carnegie.

Thomas Miller would be the first of the group to move into iron. The Prussian Kloman Brothers had developed a unique process to produce wrought iron railroad axles. These axles were forged out of scrap wrought iron. By alternatively reversing the iron during the forging process, they produced a refined grain product of superior quality. The technique is similar to the secret forging processes that gave the world Damascus and Toledo swords. Thomas Miller at the time was purchasing clerk for the Pittsburgh, Fort Wayne and Chicago

---

[9] Herbert Casson, *The Romance of Steel* (New York: A. S. Barnes & Company, 1907), 76

Railway. In this capacity, Miller was well aware of the superiority of the Kloman axle. The railroads continued to order Kloman forgings to the limit of the Kloman operation's ability to produce. Kloman came to Miller for investment money to buy a second forging hammer that could more than double the output. Miller went his friend, Henry Phipps for some additional funds. These two young men managed to get the $1600 needed and went into partnership with the Klomans in 1856. The new company became Iron City Forge. When the war broke out in 1860, axles went from two cents a pound to twelve cents a pound. Partnership problems brought in two more of the gang, Andrew and Tom Carnegie. A simple investment of $1600 in this group would have grown to one hundred million!

Iron technology and processing at Pittsburgh became world famous during the Civil War. In 1858, the Pittsburgh company of C. G. Hussey produced the first "tin plate," coating iron with corrosion-resistant tin. Prior to the Civil War, the Pittsburgh company of Piper and Shiffler was pioneering the use of iron bridges to replace wood. In 1865, Piper and Shiffler became part of the Carnegie Iron Empire taking the name, Keystone Bridge Company. Iron City Forge of the Kloman brothers was supplying the iron for these bridges. The iron bridge market was booming because of the railroad expansion. The first iron bridge west of the Alleghenies was built in the Monongahela valley in 1839 at present day Brownsville. Keystone Bridge Company would revolutionize bridge building using cast iron as well as wrought iron. The Pennsylvania railroad was a major customer and many of these iron bridges can still be seen in the Altoona, Pennsylvania, area today. In 1883, Keystone won the contract to build the superstructure for the Statue of Liberty. Keystone Bridge was a major consumer of pig iron in the world.

Still Carnegie and associates were dependent upon pig iron from outside sources in 1871. Carnegie was a believer in horizontal integration, that is, owning the full supply chain to any operation. Pig iron was a natural area for him to move into. The scene was rapidly being set for the Carnegie iron empire to develop. First coke blast furnace technology was fully developed, making Monongahela coal the prime fuel. A combination of railroads and Great Lakes shipping had opened up direct importation of Michigan iron ore. Missouri iron was available via river transportation as well. The time was right to bring iron ore to the fuel in the Monongahela valley. The firm of Kloman, Carnegie & Company and the old iron-working firm of Spang, Chalfant & Company both planned to open iron smelting blast furnace operations in Pittsburgh. In 1872, the Carnegie firm opened Lucy Furnace, named after Tom Carnegie's wife, Lucy, who was the daughter of his partner, William Coleman. At the same time Spang, Chalfant and Company opened Isabella Furnace named after a sister of one of the members. These furnaces were 75 feet high with twenty-inch bottom diameters, while of most of the nation's blast furnaces had 45-foot stacks. These heights enabled a doubling of output over the nation's competing blast furnaces. The key of course to the height of these blast furnaces was the use of coke versus charcoal, which would have never physically supported such stacks. These mighty furnaces were fed with Great Lakes ore. The rivalry of the two furnaces was legendary.

The Lucy and Isabella furnaces were tonnage machines. In their first weeks they averaged fifty tons of pig iron a day. It was noted by George Anshutz Berry, the only living relative of Pittsburgh's first furnace owner in 1793: "George Anshutz regarded forty tons a week as a magnificent work."[10] Ethan Allen of Ticonderoga fame held the early record in charcoal

---

[10] Casson, 162

furnace production at a ton every 10 hours or seventy tons a week. These furnaces, Lucy and Isabella, became known as the titans of the iron industry, making headlines around the world. In the Pittsburgh papers the tonnage battles of these furnaces appeared daily like baseball scores. The furnaces battled to 100 tons a day, averaged in 1874. The furnaces were actually meeting the Pittsburgh area's pig iron demands and were exporting to the east pig iron for the new Bessemer steel process plants in New York and Cambria.

The Lucy Furnace came under the management of Carnegie's partner and boyhood Scottish friend, Henry Phipps. Phipps was one of many of Carnegie's brilliant managers and partners. While a financier by trade, Phipps saw the need to bring science and engineering into the furnace business. Phipps was one of the first to start hiring technical people and engineers for operating positions. One of these furnace engineers was a Mr. Whitwall, who made the type of operational breakthrough that Carnegie organizations had become famous for. Phipps and Whitwall actually built a glass furnace model so they could observe the internal operation of the furnace. Experiments led to a famous recycling process that reduced ore costs and increased tonnage. A waste product of the rolling and puddling mills was flue-cinder and puddle cinder. This waste product was high in iron oxide, which was chemically like iron ore. Phipps and Whitwall started using it in Lucy Furnace with iron ore. Ultimately they were able to change to forty percent recycled flue cinder and sixty percent iron ore.[11] This greatly reduced costs and boosted productivity. This success prompted Phipps to hire the first chemist for an iron making operation, leading to a better scientific knowledge of iron making. The control of chemistry would make Lucy Furnace the premier supplier to future Bessemer steel operations.

---

[11] Bridge, 64

For Braddock, the foundry and railroad boom spurred the transportation industry. Huge amounts of coal, coke and pig iron needed to move down the Monongahela to supply Pittsburgh foundries and new iron smelting furnaces. The river traffic still had some seasonal issues so the valley was ripe for rail expansion. The Pittsburgh and Connellsville (Baltimore and Ohio) brought the rails from the east to Port Perry in 1856. In 1867, Braddock was incorporated, the Pennsylvania Railroad connected Braddock and Pittsburgh. These railroads could move coal directly from the Connellsville coke works and coalmines to Braddock and Pittsburgh. At the time of this connection the Pennsylvania Railroad's chief engineer (and future president) was J. Edgar Thomson. The superintendent of the same railroad was Andrew Carnegie. Both of these names would become forever linked with Braddock. The connection would also be a boon to Braddock's coal baron, J. B. Corey, who could ship more coal to Pittsburgh.

The railroads brought prosperity to the Monongahela valley. The iron industry of Pittsburgh depended on the railroads. Just as dependent were the railroads on the iron industry to make rails, wheels, cars and steam engines. The more you study the coal, coke, and iron business the more the history becomes one. The more you also see that one town, Braddock, became the anvil that a whole industry was forged on. In the end the railroads would be both customer and supplier to the future steel industry. Braddock would not only produce the nation's rails; it would become the spot of highest railroad traffic in the world.

Chapter 4

"Pioneering doesn't pay."

–*Andrew Carnegie*

The Sleepy Village Awakes

In the 1850s a new technology was on the horizon that would transform Braddock's Field. William Kelly invented that technology known to the Irish of Braddock as the Kelly Pneumatic Process, but to the world as the Bessemer process. That process was to light the night skies of Braddock for over 75 years. The Bessemer process was a steel making process.

I will give you a true history of the pneumatic steel making process, as a Braddock-born metallurgist and steel maker. The pneumatic steel making process (commonly now referred to as the Bessemer process) was invented by the Irish Pittsburgh steel maker, William Kelly. Kelly was at least ten years ahead of Sir Henry Bessemer in the development of the process. Kelly had been trained at the now University of Pittsburgh in metallurgy. Kelly moved to Kentucky to build and work out his process in the 1840s.

Again a little metallurgy is needed to proceed. Steel as well as wrought iron can be made from pig iron by reducing the carbon content from 3% in pig iron to .2% in the case of wrought iron and 1% or less for steel. In the previous chapter, we discussed the "heat and beat" methods used to remove carbon. The heating and beating exposes the carbon in the iron to air, which burned out the carbon. Heating and beating was a slow, labor-intensive process. Kelly as chemist was aware that air (oxygen) was actually eliminating the carbon. The heat and beat approach took cold pig iron and heated it up and then worked the iron in some method such as rolling or hammering.

The "working" exposed the surface to the air and burned the carbon out. Kelly's new process used molten (liquid) pig iron from the blast furnace. This liquid iron was then poured into a "converter" which was like a brick-lined kettle to hold the liquid. Air was then blown through the bottom of the converter by means of a tuyère. The oxygen in the air burned out the carbon directly. The process produced a fountain of sparks and light that could be seen for miles. While he probably had the process developed by late 1849, Kelly did not apply for a patent until 1852. Kelly clearly defined the chemistry of the process, which Bessemer used to develop the supporting equipment. Bessemer engineering allowed for English mills to adopt the process far ahead of the Americans. Ultimately Bessemer won the legal battle, but as an Englishman, he never earned the credit of the American Irish.

With that basic metallurgical note, Sir Henry Bessemer described the process eloquently: "The powerful jets of air spring upward through the fluid mass of metal. The air expanding in volume divides itself into globules, or bursts violently upward, carrying with it some hundredweight of fluid metal, which again falls into the boiling mass below. Every part of the apparatus trembles under the violent agitation thus produced; a roaring flame rushes from the mouth of the vessel, and as the process advances it changes its violet color to orange, and finally to a voluminous pure white flame."[1]

In 1860, Captain E. B. Ward of Detroit licensed the Kelly pneumatic process and the Bessemer equipment. Daniel Morrell of Johnstown was part of the company that built this first pneumatic steel plant in Wyandotte, Michigan. Morrell had come from the Cambria Iron Company of Johnstown, which was famous for the production of wrought iron railroad rails. While the Detroit plant was to produce structural steel,

---

[1] Bridge, 145

the hope was to break into the steel rail business. The first Kelly (Bessemer) steel was rolled on 1864. The plant used the machinery invented by Henry Bessemer, who had independently "invented" the pneumatic steel process in England. Railroads were just starting to experiment with steel rails in 1867, but the future market was huge. The miles of railroads increased in 1864 from 33908 miles to 77740 miles in 1874.

In 1864, a rival Bessemer rail plant was built in Troy, New York. This plant used the full Bessemer patent and was designed by engineer Alexander L. Holley. This Troy plant was actually partially owned by the Pennsylvania Railroad. While Kelly ultimately lost the patent battle and name, he was the inventor of the process while Bessemer should rightly be called the inventor of the machinery. It was the chemical genius of Kelly that hypothesized the reactions. For decades, the Irish of Braddock refused to refer to the process as Bessemer, calling it the Kelly converter. I totally agree that Kelly was the inventor of the "Bessemer" process but for simplicity I will use the name Bessemer throughout the book.

Actually Cambria Iron Company in Johnstown claims to have rolled the first steel rails for railroad rails in 1855.[2] This was probably an experimental batch for the Pennsylvania Railroad and its manager Edgar Thomson. This rail steel was either made by a special "heat and beat" method or was made from a very limited batch of crucible steel. In any case it was not Bessemer steel. The first trials in 1862 of steel rails by the Pennsylvania Railroad under then president Edgar Thomson was with crucible steel. Cambria would roll the first Bessemer rails in the United States in 1867. The Bessemer ingots were made at a Bessemer plant in Steelton, Pennsylvania, and rolled at Cambria.

---

[2] Lewis C. Walkinshaw, *Annals of Southwestern Pennsylvania* (New York: Lewis Historical Publishing, 1939), 136

Another metallurgical minute is needed to understand crucible steel. Crucible steel is made by heating pig iron in ceramic crucibles in a gas or coal fired furnace. The crucible is heated for days. The very long heating slowly burns the carbon out of the pig iron, producing steel. Remember that steel can range from a tenth of a percent carbon to one percent carbon. The crucible process is not only slow but can only reduce carbon to the two to three tenths percent carbon for rails. Crucible steel's higher carbon content means a more brittle steel. The Pennsylvania Railroad learned this the hard way with the breaking of some of the rails in service. Winter temperatures make steel even more brittle so the winter was particularly hard on crucible steel. The Pennsylvania Railroad studies, however, did note the high wear on these first experimental rails, but believed the future would be steel if its toughness could be improved. Another problem of crucible steel was it cost almost ten times as much as Bessemer steel.

Bessemer steel was made by blowing air through the molten pig iron. The Bessemer converter vomited a steady stream of sparks. As a Pittsburgher, the night skies are legendary for their brightness and orange color from Bessemer converters. Carnegie historian, John Bridge, observed: "the chemical changes accompanying this gorgeous display are equally beautiful." The fountain of sparks became a snow of iron dust throughout the Monongahela valley. I can remember well the need to sweep this dust off porches every morning. The Bessemers would also put a heavy smell of rotten eggs throughout the valley (sulfur). In locations like Bessemer Terrace on the hill above Edgar Thomson, the dust could be a quarter inch thick!

Another great description of what the environment looked like comes from a young Charles Schwab (future Carnegie partner and first president of USS). As a boy, Schwab lived twenty miles northeast of Johnstown's Cambria plant. Schwab described his view of Johnstown: "Along toward dusk tongues of flame would shoot up in the pall around Johnstown. When some furnace door was opened the evening turned red. A boy watching from the rim of the hills had a vast arena before him, a place of vague forms, great labors, and dancing fires. And the murk always present, the smell of the foundry. It gets into your hair, your clothes, even your blood."[3] This is a description that I so well remember as a Pittsburgh boy. The smell of sulfur was to any steel town the smell of prosperity.

The amount of carbon removed by the Bessemer process depended on the length of the air "blow." This air blow was from fifteen to twenty minutes. The converter operator watched the amount and nature of the sparks to estimate the amount of carbon removed. With enough time and air, the carbon could be lowered to the low level of wrought iron. For good rail steel, two-tenths percent carbon content was ideal. A two-tenths percent carbon (.2%) produced the right amount of toughness, strength and wear resistance. This last point presented a minor technical problem, for even the Bessemer process had variation. Carbon controls in steel making as well as oxygen control were major problems. Over-blowing would reduce the carbon below the optimum two-tenths percent and that in turn reduced wear and strength. In addition, over-blowing increased the oxygen content in the steel. This oxygen in the steel, if not removed, made the steel brittle. Bessemer had learned this early on as he produced tons of bad steel.

The answer came in 1857 by the work of another metallurgist, Mr. Robert Mushet. Mushet added a type of manganese ore (spiegeleisen) to the molten iron, which had solved the problem of brittleness caused by too much oxygen. The manganese cleaned the steel of the oxygen. Actually this

---

[3] David McCullough, *The Johnstown Flood* (New York: Touchstone Books, 1986), 23

approach was used earlier in Prussia to produce high quality steel. While Mushet was looking to control carbon and oxygen in steel, serendipity played a role in improved steel properties. Because the spiegeleisen was extremely high in the element manganese, during the Bessemer process it added manganese to the steel. Future metallurgists were to find that manganese strengthened and toughened steel in its own right. In addition it helped tie up the tramp element, sulfur. The fact is, without Mushet's invention, neither Kelly nor Bessemer could produce rail steel. About fifteen minutes to twenty minutes of blow was needed to convert ten tons of pig iron into Bessemer steel with the Mushet invention.

There are some other metallurgical fine points that can cause poor Bessemer steel for rails. One of these caused the failure of the Freedom Iron and Steel Works of Lewistown, Pennsylvania. This plant, unlike the plants of Johnstown, Pittsburgh and Detroit used eastern iron ore, which is naturally high in phosphorus. Phosphorus is a trace element that can embrittle steel. Worse yet the Bessemer process is incapable of removing it. The smelter could not control phosphorous at the time. The amount in steel was a result of the ore and coke phosphorus content going into the furnace. Freedom Iron failed in 1868 but was dismantled and reassembled in Joliet, Illinois. The rebuilt furnace worked successfully then with low phosphorus ore from the Great Lakes region, which was also being used at Edgar Thomson Works. Through all these industry failures and failed product trials, Edgar Thomson, president of the Pennsylvania Railroad, kept a vision of the potential of Bessemer steel rails.

Cambria Iron Company did not erect its first Bessemer converter until 1869 and the first Bessemer rails were rolled in 1871. Cambria did however hire Kelly to experiment with pneumatic steel making at the plant in 1858. It was at Cambria that Kelly became famous in the steel business. Cambria Iron

The Sleepy Village Awakes

Company as we shall see was in every way the father of Braddock and its future Edgar Thomson Steel Works.

Railroad rails had evolved from wood to cast iron to wrought iron to steel. Cast iron offered the greatest wear resistance because of its high carbon content. Cast iron was strong and could handle the load but was brittle to mechanical shock. Wrought iron with its extremely low carbon content would handle the shock of heavy, fast moving trains. Wrought iron, which is as close to pure iron as it gets, was a bit too soft, however, for heavy railroad traffic. This softness could cause "snaking" which led to many wrecks. Wrought iron also wore faster than cast iron. In the 1850s steel was an unknown engineering material. Steel had been made by forging in swords and tools. However, it was not a tonnage product. Like anything new, there were many concerns from the railroaders. Pittsburgh and Braddock were lucky to have a pioneering spirit in Edgar Thomson and a great salesman in Andrew Carnegie. Neither were technical men or engineers. Still each was a true businessman. Without the railroads there was no significant market for steel except maybe bridges.

Carnegie was a visionary in seeing the future of steel in bridges. Carnegie did have some experience in rolling of puddled steel at his Union Mills operation, which supplied his Keystone Bridge Company. Keystone in 1870 supplied the superstructure for the Eads Bridge in St. Louis. Finished in 1874, it was the first steel bridge. It remains in use today and was the first use of chromium to alloy iron and steel. At the time the 520-foot span across the Ohio River was the longest in existence.

Initially Andrew Carnegie showed no interest in the production of Bessemer steel. It violated a basic Carnegie rule of "never pioneering," however, two partners of Carnegie were extremely interested in Bessemer production: Tom Carnegie (Andrew's younger brother) and William Coleman.

Tom Carnegie was Coleman's son-in-law and Homewood neighbor. Coleman and Tom Carnegie used to drive from Homewood to downtown Pittsburgh together every day. Tom Carnegie, with his lovable personality, was the dealmaker.

John Bridge, Andrew Carnegie's longtime secretary, felt the concept of the future Edgar Thomson Works was worked out between Coleman and Tom Carnegie during these many drives downtown to work. William Coleman was an amazing Pittsburgh capitalist. Born in New York, he came to Pittsburgh as an apprentice bricklayer. In 1845, he started a forge and rolling mill to make wagon axles. In the 1860s using these profits he successfully invested in coalmines in Irwin, Pennsylvania. He further invested in oil wells north of Pittsburgh. In 1863, Coleman opened an iron rail rolling mill in Sharon, Pennsylvania. Besides these iron and rolling mill investments, Coleman was partnering in railroads such as the Allegheny Valley railroad. Coleman visited Europe in 1867 to study coke, rail rolling and the Bessemer process. Upon return from Europe, he made a trip to the Great Lakes iron ore mines. It is clear that no man in Pittsburgh better understood the railroad rail business and the Bessemer process. I firmly believe historian John Bridge to be correct that William Coleman was the visionary of Edgar Thomson Works.

Another Carnegie railroad friend and Homewood neighbor, John Scott, was also convinced of the future in Bessemer steel rails. Trials on the Allegheny railroad had shown the amazing wear resistance and load handling of Bessemer steel. John Scott was director of the Allegheny Valley Railroad. Finally, Colonel Thomas Scott, director of the Pennsylvania Railroad and former Carnegie boss also believed strongly in the use of Bessemer rails. Carnegie partners, Coleman, Phipps and Tom Carnegie were early believers in the future of Bessemer steel. Coleman in particular had spent years studying the possibilities of Bessemer and was eager to invest in it.

Coleman and Phipps got some other key people interested in the application of Bessemer rail steel. One of these was David McCandless, vice-president of the Exchange National Bank. McCandless was heavily invested in the coalfields and saw this as a future boom in the growth of railroads. McCandless was also the financial man of the group, having the best education and experience in finance. Another member of what Andrew Carnegie called the "young geniuses" was David Stewart. Stewart was president of the Pittsburgh Locomotive Works and a director of the Allegheny Valley railroad. Amazingly Coleman, Scott, McCandless and Tom Carnegie were all neighbors. Andrew Carnegie had made much from these friendships in the past but he was also slow to get into the Bessemer steel business. Carnegie liked to research and listen to many different views. He was a very conservative investor. He hated to pioneer but wanted to be what marketing people call an "early adopter."

The story of how Andrew Carnegie came to build the great Edgar Thomson Bessemer steel plant was typical of his luck. In England by 1870, the use of Bessemer steel for rails was booming. Scott talked the then president of the Pennsylvania Railroad, Edgar Thomson, into sending Andrew Carnegie to Europe to sell bonds. Of course, while there Andrew could also look into and study the Bessemer steel industry. Once in Europe, Andrew did exactly that: he launched a major study of Bessemer steel making. In 1872, Carnegie actually visited Henry Bessemer at his Sheffield Steelworks. Bessemer had been very successful in England, with over twenty Bessemer steel plants in operation. Carnegie was taken in by the salesmanship of the then fifty-nine-year-old metallurgist. One of Bessemer's favorite sales tools was an old cannon cast out of his steel. That cannon had demonstrated the strength of his new steel. Still Germany's great Krupp Works had rejected the Bessemer process, favoring the new "open-hearth" process.

Carnegie needed an explanation of why the Bessemer steel process had not had the same success in the great steel mills of Germany?

Bessemer's story included the secret of Germany's rejection of the process. Bessemer was an inventor, a chemist and a metallurgist. It was his scientific knowledge that had gained him success. Like Kelly he had faced many early failures. In particular, Bessemer's early experiments produced very brittle steel. Analysis of the steel showed a high phosphorous content, which caused brittle steel. This started him on a sidetrack of trying to remove the phosphorous in the furnace. Bessemer found that his source of phosphorus was from the English ores used to make the pig iron used in the Bessemer furnace. The break that commercialized the Bessemer process came when Swedish iron ores, which are extremely low in phosphorus, came on the market. These low phosphorous ores made end product steel very ductile. The Germans did not have a source of low phosphorus ores, which ended the use of Bessemer steel in Germany. Again Carnegie's oldest partner, Providence, joined him again, for the new Great Lakes ores being used in Pittsburgh were extremely low in phosphorus.

Carnegie was also able to view Bessemer rails that had been in service over fifteen years in Europe and showing little wear. Besides the science and technology, which Carnegie saw, he saw the future. England had a booming Bessemer industry and Bessemer steel production no longer fit the concept of pioneering; it was already a success in Europe. At the same time his partner William Coleman was touring a very successful Bessemer plant only fifty miles from Pittsburgh: the Cambria Iron Company. Coleman's tour of Cambria was one of a series of American Bessemer plants he visited. In reality the main startup problems of producing Bessemer were well behind on the industry learning curve. There were already seven Bessemer steel plants in the United States when Carnegie returned from Europe.

The proposition of building a Bessemer steel rail plant now became a necessity to the investor Carnegie. Carnegie had seen the huge profits of the English steel making operations. He had talked to Sir Bessemer himself and had proven the process. Carnegie had also seen the outstanding performance of the rails on the roads. Edgar Thomson, the president of America's major railroad believed in the future of Bessemer rails. In addition other railroad presidents such as Thomas Scott believed in it. All his friends believed in its future. In addition the building of a Bessemer steel plant would be a huge customer for his pig iron production at Lucy Furnace. Carnegie returned determined to build a plant.

While Carnegie was in Europe, his partners Coleman, Scott, McCandless and Tom Carnegie were looking for a plant site. On January 1, 1873 William Coleman purchased the option on Braddock's Field. With Carnegie's support a partnership was formed which purchased parts of the venture. Andrew Carnegie originally was not the major investor but the new firm was named Carnegie, McCandless & Company. The partnership included Coleman, Kloman, Phipps, McCandless, Scott, Stewart, Tom Carnegie and Shinn. Coleman brought in William Shinn but he was never part of Carnegie's inner group. Still Shinn had the strongest managerial experience, having worked a number of supervisory jobs for the Pittsburgh, Fort Wayne and Chicago Railroad. Originally Coleman put $10,000 into the new firm, while the others contributed $50,000 each. A friend of the partners described it as: "Shinn bossed the show; McCandless lent it dignity; Phipps took in the pennies at the gate and kept the payroll down; Tom Carnegie kept everybody in a good humor; and Andy looked after advertising and beating the bandwagon."[4]

---

[4] Casson, 85

The newly converted Andrew Carnegie would sell the nation on Bessemer steel.

The strength of Carnegie's partnership was friendship. Many of them were boyhood friendships such as boyhood slum mate, Henry Phipps. Andrew Carnegie said, "My partners are not only partners, but a band of devoted friends, who never have a difference. I have never had to exercise my power, and of this I am very proud. I never enjoyed anything more than to get a sound thrashing in an argument at the hands of these young geniuses." Carnegie built a natural business network around his friends and partners, who became his suppliers and customers as well.

Andrew Carnegie was thirty-eight years old at the time at the time of the purchase of Braddock's Field. It was Carnegie who required the new plant be named after his old friend, mentor and future customer, Edgar Thomson, president of the Pennsylvania Railroad. With the finances set, it was Carnegie's vision that would make Edgar Thomson Works famous. Carnegie did every thing in a world-class manner. While other steel makers built steel mills to be competitive and efficient, Carnegie's mission was to be the best in the world.

Braddock needed more than the processes of Kelly and Bessemer, the railroads of Edgar Thomson, and the finances of Carnegie; it needed engineering genius. Steel had to take over the wrought iron steel market in rails. To that end Carnegie hired the best Bessemer engineer in the world, Alexander Holley. Holley in 1862 had visited the Bessemer steelworks at Sheffield. Holley was an exceptional metallurgist, engineer and a prolific technical writer. Holley had built most of the operating Bessemer mills in this country, in particular two of the best and world-class plants at Troy and Cambria. Other than possibly Henry Bessemer, there was no better person to build Carnegie's dream. In typical Carnegie fashion, Holley was given a free hand to build the best operating mill possible. The plant was to be a two six-ton converter mill capable of 75000 tons of Bessemer steel per year.

The first problem was the Great Panic of 1873, which caused a shortage of investment capital. This was, with the exception of the Depression, the biggest financial panic in the United States and the world. Carnegie depended on his own wealth to carry him through the difficult years. Banks questioned Carnegie's loans and hesitated to supply money. The railroads were near bankruptcy. It is said, "Unemployment shot to 25 percent, forcing men, women and children to beg in the streets. Carnegie had to circumnavigate the lines outside thirty-four soup kitchens feeding five to seven thousand daily."[5] Carnegie's dream would have been lost if it wasn't for the high standing of McCandless, Stewart and Scott with the Pittsburgh banking community. The status of these men brought in a loan from New York banker, J. P. Morgan. Clearly each of these young geniuses had a specific role in the Edgar Thomson Works.

The future of Braddock's Edgar Thomson Works would determine the future of the American steel industry. No place on earth would produce as much Bessemer steel as Braddock, Pennsylvania. In manufacturing heavy gauge and light gauge rails from 1875 to 1913, Edgar Thomson Works would produce enough rails to lay track to the moon and back several times! By 2004 it can be said that no plant on the face of the earth has produced as much steel as Edgar Thomson Works. Today Edgar Thomson Works has the last operating blast furnace in the once great Monongahela Steel Valley.

---

[5] Peter Krass, *Carnegie* (Hoboken, New Jersey: John Wiley, 2002), 120

Chapter 5

"—A light that flung violet shadows everywhere and made the gray outside rain a beautiful blue. A fountain of sparks arose, gorgeous as ten thousand rockets, and fell with a beautiful curve, like the petals of some enormous flower."
—*Bessemer Description in McClure's 1893*

"ET"–Edgar Thomson Works

The Edgar Thomson Works was built on the exact site of the defeat of the British under General Braddock. By the end of the 1870s this site would again deliver a crushing blow to Britain. By the end the 1870s decade, Edgar Thomson Works would humble the proud and world dominant British steel industry. As one historian put it: "Braddock became the Mecca of iron and steel manufacturers the world over." In six years, Edgar Thomson Works smashed every type of production and productivity record held by the British steel industry. If history were ever to record the seven wonders of the Industrial Revolution, Edgar Thomson Works would be there with Edison's Laboratory and Henry Ford's first auto plant. By 1882 a bewildered British steel association was making offers for the "boys of Braddock" to come over and explain how to make Bessemer steel. With the closing of Cambria Steel Company in 1992, Edgar Thomson Works is today the oldest steel plant in America still in operation. Since its conception, Edgar Thomson Works has made and processed more steel than any other plant on earth. Its managerial ranks would produce over fifty millionaires and over thirty industrial company presidents in all types of American industries. Some of these large corporate presidencies were United States Steel, Bethlehem Steel, International Nickel, Mesta Machine and over sixty smaller firms.

Even more firsts can be attributed to Braddock's industrial jewel. Edgar Thomson would be the birthplace of manufacturing cost accounting, industrial chemistry and as process control. The managerial practices would be the textbook for future generations of steel makers and manufacturers. Besides cost accounting, Edgar Thomson Works pioneered personnel and human resource management. "Throughput" speed was a hallmark of Edgar Thomson and predated many "Just in Time" techniques of today. Edgar Thomson Works would pioneer the concept of quick tooling change over, which is today the heart of the Japanese success in on time delivery. Edgar Thomson Works like Braddock's Defeat became the training ground for the future managers. Most of the great steel makers and industrialists of the twenty-first century had to pass through Braddock. Braddock was front-page news on the business pages for decades. In the *American Manufacturer* of October 4, 1889, a reporter declared, *"The superintendency of the Edgar Thomson plant demanded greater executive capacity than the presidency of the United States."*

The industrial site of the plant was to be on the major part of the fiercest and bloodiest fighting on Braddock's Field. The ground was sacred ground for our nation. That tradition would continue, as on the site of Edgar Thomson Works, thousands of men would lose their lives and be injured in mill accidents on this ground. Carnegie's greatest manager would fall on this very spot as well. Furthermore it would be the location of one of the first deaths in the steel labor movements.

At the time of the purchase of Braddock's Field, it still had only a handful of farmers and miners as residents. The purchased land was described as one hundred and seven acres of farmland. Both the Pennsylvania Railroad and the Baltimore & Ohio Railroad cut through the property. It also had the Monongahela River on its southern borders. While Carnegie was in Europe studying the Bessemer process, his brother Tom and William Coleman remained confident that they had the right location even though Carnegie was not interested in a steel making plant when he left for Europe. Braddock's Field was a textbook site having rail and river transportation. Carnegie found the Bessemer religion in Europe and returned with enthusiasm. Carnegie showed his commitment to the Braddock area in his *Autobiography*: "Tom, you and Mr. Coleman are right about the location; right at Braddock's, between the Pennsylvania, the Baltimore and Ohio, and the river, is the best situation in America; and let's call the works after our dear friend Edgar Thomson. Let us go over to Mr. Coleman's and drive out to Braddock's."[1] Carnegie was well versed in the history of Braddock's Field. He talked of the two Scottish soldiers of his hometown, Dunfermline, Scotland: "it was there that the then provost of Dunfermline, Sir Arthur Halkett, and his son were slain." These native sons had been part of Braddock's Coldstream Guards. Carnegie when on to note that: "It was a coincidence that what had been a field of death to two native-born citizens of Dunfermline should be turned into an industrial hive by two others."[2] Even more amazing is that a plant manager of Edgar Thomson Works in 1892, Thomas Morrison, would be from Dunfermline, Scotland.

Carnegie also had Edgar Thomson's endorsement that there was no better location. Having agreement Carnegie and his associates went on to buy farmland from a Mr. McKinney. An extremely cold winter delayed the original start of

---

[1] Andrew Carnegie, *The Autobiography of Andrew Carnegie* (Boston: Northeastern University Press, 1920), 180
[2] ibid., 181

construction. Ground was broken for Edgar Thomson Works on April 13, 1873. Alexander Holley was in charge of its design. Phineas Barnes was in charge of construction. Phineas Barnes had built the Joliet Bessemer plant. Again we see that Carnegie brought only the best men he could find to the project. As might be expected initial construction turned up bones and artifacts of the battle of Braddock. Peter Krass in his book, *Carnegie,* noted: "After the spring thaw, excavations for the mill's foundations were started at once, during which the men uncovered numerous relics from Braddock's 1755 battle including bayonets and swords."[3] Many of these artifacts can still be seen today in Braddock's Carnegie Library.

The hiring of Alexander Holley was typical of Carnegie's world-class approach to Edgar Thomson Works from the start. Holley was an engineer and graduate of Brown University. During his college years he received his first patent for a steam engine cut-off valve. Ultimately he held over 15 patents, mostly on Bessemer process equipment. He wrote over 300 articles on engineering, something that closet writer Andrew Carnegie admired. Holley's book on the manufacture of armor and ordnance was considered a standard textbook throughout the world. In a 1947 tribute to Holley, *Mechanical Engineering* magazine noted: "Holley's greatness as an engineer lay in his talent to comprehend the utility of things and in his ability to gather and digest facts and theories bearing on any engineering problem, without prejudice to any side of the question, and to reach with almost unerring accuracy a true evaluation of a new idea or development."

Holley's experience was unequaled. In the 1860s he toured the great Bessemer plants of England. He was able to work directly with Sir Henry Bessemer. Holley gained the rights to license the Bessemer process in the United States. Holley was

---

[3] Krass, 119

an excellent engineer capable of making the plant happen. He had built the great Bessemer leviathans at Troy, Steelton, Joliet and Johnstown (Cambria). Holley did not just copy his earlier works but innovated and improved. Steel historian, Casson, noted the following on Holley's Edgar Thomson design: "In arranging these works, Mr. Holley made many improvements over any of his previous efforts, and, assisted as he was (Mr. P. Barnes, resident engineer, and Mr. Jones), the works stand today as a fit monument of the progress of the Bessemer process in this country." One of the improvements he implemented at Edgar Thomson was the use of a design that allowed for quick relining of the Bessemer converter. The refractory brick that lined the converter wore down with each heat of steel made. The converter then had to be taken out of production and relined. Holley's design allowed for a back-up quick-change converter vessel. This design allowed for the continuous flow of steel. This would be one of several improvements that would give Edgar Thomson Works every major steel making record over the next twenty years and hold many of them over the next fifty. It is amazing that the Japanese a hundred years later would apply the same quick-changeover systems to automotive tooling. Like Holley's application at Edgar Thomson, quick-change tooling allows for continuous production even when car models vary. Edgar Thomson Works can rightfully claim the birthplace of quick-change tooling in the invention of the Holley trunnion system. It should be noted that after the construction of Edgar Thomson Works, Holley converted the Pittsburgh steel mill of Jones and Laughlin to a Bessemer plant.

The original plan for the mill called for two six-ton Bessemer converters with projected capacity of 225 tons per day. This was almost twice the capacity of Cambria, which had two three-ton converters. Originally Carnegie even planned for two open-hearth furnaces to produce very special quality steel.[4] The market for Bessemer steel had grown from 3000 tons in 1867 to 375,517 tons in 1875 when Edgar Thomson opened. In addition the mill would need a cupola furnace to melt pig iron from Pittsburgh's Lucy Furnace and steel scrap generated in the Edgar Thomson rolling mills. This lack of blast furnaces was an initial design inefficiency. Edgar Thomson Works would lack blast furnaces to supply liquid pig iron to the Bessemer converter depending on re-melted cupola pig iron. Of course the operating inefficiency at Edgar Thomson Works was offset by full utilization of Carnegie's other operations such as Lucy Furnace.

Another metallurgical minute is required. A Bessemer converter is a large pear shaped kettle or pot. Its outside is a steel frame but it is lined with refractory brick. The refractory brick contains the liquid pig iron in the vessel as well as the high heat. The vessel (kettle) is slipped onto a large steel ring called a trunnion, which allows the converter to be tilled and removed to reline bricks. The trunnion ring allowed for a vessel to be put in very quickly with a crane. If you are lucky enough to visit western Pennsylvania, you can see a converter preserved at Station Square on the south side of Pittsburgh. The liquid pig iron would come from a cupola or blast furnace and be poured into the ladle, which by crane went to the Bessemer converter. The liquid pig iron was then poured into the Bessemer converter. A blast (blow) of air would then be blown through the bottom of the vessel. Once the carbon was removed, making steel, it would be poured in into ingot molds. In plants in Cambria, Troy and Detroit, blast furnaces could supply liquid pig iron to the converter.

In the case of Edgar Thomson Works, cold pig was shipped by railroad from Lucy Furnace. Edgar Thomson Works also purchased a small amount of pig on the open world market. A cupola was then used to re-melt the cold pig iron to produce

---

[4] Stubbles, 32

liquid iron for the Bessemer converter. A cupola is a stack similar to a blast furnace. Pig iron and coke are added in layers. Air is blown in, melting the pig iron. Because of the high carbon content and the refined nature of the added pig iron, the cupola operates at much lower temperatures than blast furnaces, generating much more liquid per hour than a blast furnace. The cupola can also re-melt scrap steel that was generated in the blooming and rolling processes.

The movement of cold pig iron by railroad was not a problem. Braddock already had two railroads running through it, the Pennsylvania Railroad and the Baltimore & Ohio Railroad. By 1890, Braddock would be a connection center for the five greatest railroads in the country, adding Pittsburgh & Lake Erie, Bessemer & Lake Erie and the Western Maryland. What made this more important was that Carnegie created a business concept of cooperative advantage. He had forged a business partnership that made the railroads both suppliers and customers. As a customer the railroads would favor Edgar Thomson Bessemer steel because it would mean business for them. In fact it allowed for reduced freight rates to the Edgar Thomson Works. In addition Carnegie had weaved a financial network of interlocking ties with the railroads. The railroad success became tied to Carnegie Steel's success. Finally Carnegie's naming the mill after the president of the Pennsylvania Railroad was marketing genius.

At Edgar Thomson Works the pig iron was melted to liquid, then it was poured from the cupola into a ladle to be taken to the egg-shaped Bessemer converter. Once in the converter, air was blown through the liquid metal. As the air burned out the carbon, the flame color and sparks change. The change of color and sparks allowed the operator to estimate the amount of carbon in the liquid steel. The light would be seen for miles. It is a ten- to twenty-minute intense process of sparks, light, and noise. Nineteenth-century writers described as, "A thunder of cannons and a burst of spluttering flakes of fire." Temperatures in the converter reach temperatures of over 3000 degrees. This liquid temperature causes a light so intense that, like an eclipse or when arc welding, thick, colored eyeglasses are required to look at it.

Another description of the Braddock Bessemers was made around 1990 by a Braddock writer/poet:

> "Where the cannon of Braddock were wheeled into the line,
> There the turning converter, while roaring flame,
> Pours out cascades of comets and showers of stars,
> While the pulpit-boy, goggled, looks into the same-
> Thinking little of Braddock and nothing of Mars."[5]

For many workers it was too intense. Still a group of the Irish seemed to thrive in this environment of awe and fear. At the end of the process, spiegeleisen (ferromanganese) was added as "softener" and "cleaner." The converted steel was then poured into iron molds to cool the steel into a large solid ingot. An ingot can be eight to fourteen feet high and weigh several tons to ninety tons each.

On August 22, 1875, Edgar Thomson's first heat of liquid Bessemer steel was produced. The product of that heat was 2200 rails for the Pennsylvania Railroad. By 1879, Edgar Thomson Works held world records in tonnage for a day, week and year. Edgar Thomson Works was out-producing most all the world's countries. Profits for a year surpassed one and half million dollars per year.

Since the last Bessemer blew in this country in 1959, the reader may ask how it relates to the now used "basic oxygen process." The basic difference is that pure oxygen is used instead of air (20% oxygen). Basic oxygen furnaces run hotter

---

[5] John P. Hoerr, *And the Wolf Finally Came* (Pittsburgh: University of Pittsburgh Press, 1988), 168

and faster. The chemistry of burning carbon out of the pig iron remains the same. They are free of the trademark sparks of the Bessemer process as well as the bright flames. The goal, however, is the same, to remove carbon from pig iron and convert it to steel. Personally I miss the beauty of the orange night skies and the sparks that made one historian note: "This is the Bessemer converter, the most beautiful and perfect piece of mechanism ever devised by the human mind." There are still some Bessemer converters working in the Ural Mountains of Russia.

After iron was converted to steel ingots and cooled, solid ingots are then taken cold or preferably hot to rolling/blooming mill soaking pits to bring the metal back to a rolling temperature around 1800 degrees. The ingot is then rolled on the blooming mill, which is an intermediate process, or rolling that makes a "bloom." A bloom is roughly a 12-inch by 12-inch beam of steel that is cut to lengths of 12 to 16 feet. Blooming mills were behemoth pieces of equipment powered by massive steam engines. Once the bloom was created it was moved to the finishing mill reheat furnaces to bring the steel temperature to a finish rolling temperature. The finishing mill rolled the railroad rails. If we look at one of the first months of full production, January 1876, Edgar Thomson Works blew 433 converter batches of pig iron. From these 433 heats (the term for a batch of converter product), 2550 tons of ingots were produced. From this, 2055 tons of rails were produced. Again huge steam engines were required to power these mills. One description at the time: "I saw men prodding in the deep soaking pits where ingots glowed in white hot chambers. I saw other men in the hot yellow glare from the furnaces. It was a place into which men went like men going into war for the sake of wives and children, urged on by necessity. A man works in peril of his life for 14 cents an hour, upon such toil rests the splendor of American civilization."

In the difficult economic times of the 1870s that Edgar Thomson Works opened, these intermediate steel blooms were also being sold direct to other steel processing plants to be rolled into other products because of the poor rail market. Carnegie pioneered new markets for Bessemer steel blooms. Some steel blooms were sold to forge shops to make axles. Agricultural implement forging markets were also found. In 1879, Carnegie won for Edgar Thomson Works the contract to supply the structural steel for the Brooklyn Bridge. The minister who dedicated the Brooklyn Bridge stated of the Edgar Thomson steel, "the chiefest of the instruments, the kindliest instrument of peoples for subduing the earth."

In the next few years, Carnegie the salesmen, would find more applications for Braddock steel. Two huge orders came again from New York to build the Hudson River Bridge and the New York Subway as well as the Statue of Liberty. In addition a huge rail order for the Canadian Pacific came in.

Steam was the power source of these huge Bessemer plants. The steam generation actually caused some usual natural occurrences for those living near the mill. On extremely cold January nights, like those noted by George Washington in the Monongahela valley, the mill caused snows in nearby neighborhoods such as North Braddock, East Pittsburgh and Turtle Creek. These snows came from the high and hot humidity of steam generation. As it went up from the mill it became snow. On a clear cold night, white-out localized snows could occur. These snows are like the "lake effect" snows known by many in winters around the Great Lakes.

When Edgar Thomson Works started, Braddock's population was mainly Irish, Scots-Irish, German, and some minor numbers of Austrians, English, Welsh and Blacks. The opening and success of the great Cambria Bessemer plant in Johnstown had started a new flow of laborers into western

Pennsylvania. The new immigration was of Italians, Poles, Russians and Hungarians. The native residents referred to all these new foreigners as "bohunks" or "hunkies." There was a great deal of tension between the natives and the "foreigners." The small town soon had its Irish sections, German sections etc.

The equipment was no doubt impressive but Carnegie knew that men, not equipment, were the largest component of productivity. William Shinn was the Carnegie partner assigned as general manager. One of the first things he addressed was the development of an excellent cost accounting system. This was at Carnegie's request because he had noticed it was lacking in most steel making operations. Cost accounting is not the most exciting development but it was the foundation of improvement. Most historians of the plant and industry have underestimated the contribution of Shinn's accounting. Accounting was one of the few business courses that Andrew Carnegie had taken as a young boy. Carnegie was extremely interested in the development of a cost system at Edgar Thomson. This outstanding accounting system allowed for a continuous assault on the costs of manufacturing. In Carnegie's study of the iron and steel industry he was amazed at the lack of cost accounting. Carnegie noted in his *Autobiography:* "I was greatly surprised to find that the cost of each of the various processes was unknown. Inquiries made of the leading manufacturers of Pittsburgh proved this. It was a lump business, and until stock was taken and the books balanced at the end of the year, the manufacturers were in total ignorance of the results. I heard of men who thought their business at the end of year would show a loss and had found a profit, and vice versa." Edgar Thomson Works would be totally different on the American scene. At the new works every detail of each of the processes would be known. Shinn was also an aggressive cost cutter. Shinn's specific process-oriented accounting allowed managers to focus in on areas where costs could be reduced. Shinn's accounting system and cost cutting played into Carnegie belief to invest in new equipment when necessary to reduce costs.

As part of this new accounting system, weight scales were installed at points throughout the process. Shinn could then calculate losses at various stages of the operation. It was an approach to waste that would be used eventually throughout the industry. The savings that came from merely understanding the losses were huge. Carnegie recorded its success: "One of the chief sources of success in manufacturing is the introduction and strict maintenance of a perfect system of accounting so that responsibility for money or materials can be brought home to every man. Owners who, in the office, would not trust a clerk with five dollars without having a check on him, were supplying tons of material daily to men in the mills without exacting an account of their stewardship by weighing what each returned in finished form."[6]

These outstanding accounting systems of Edgar Thomson Works led to the addition of a blast furnace in1879. At startup most of the pig iron came from the Carnegie controlled Lucy Furnaces. Shinn correctly saw that this was an additional cost to the rails that could be reduced. These costs were substantial, involving producing the pig iron at Lucy Furnaces, then transporting it to Edgar Thomson, only to re-melt it again in a cupola for use in the Bessemer converter. He convinced other partners that a blast furnace could significantly reduce costs. Shinn and plant manager, Bill Jones, then hired the best furnace engineer in the country, Julian Kennedy. This led to the purchase of an Escanaba, Michigan charcoal furnace that was dismantled and sent to Braddock. Kennedy and Jones took this old charcoal furnace and made it a world-class, state

---

[6] Harold Livesay, *Andrew Carnegie* (Boston: Little, Brown and Company, 1975), 85

of the art blast furnace for Edgar Thomson Works. This single furnace was blown in on January 1880 and within a few months was outperforming any of the Lucy furnaces. It was so successful that a second furnace was added at Edgar Thomson Works in 1882.

Edgar Thomson furnace records continued into the next century. The world was in awe of the steel making of Braddock. In the 1880s, John Morely, the great parliamentarian and statesman visited Edgar Thomson Works with the following observation: "I visited the Carnegie Steel Works this week, and have visited many works in my own country, but I believe the iron and steel manufacturers of England who are with me and who have been here several days, will concur with me when I say that these are the most stupendous steel works to be seen in any country in the world. The huge triumphs of the ironmasters of Pittsburgh in the production of steel, can only be told in colossal figures that are almost as hard to realize in our minds as the figures of astronomical distances or geologic time."

Steel historian Casson used the analogy of a naval fleet to describe the history of Carnegie and the formation of the United States Steel Corporation. Casson developed the following historical analogy: "Leading the way came the warships, the most formidable navy in the world. Admiral Schwab stands on the deck of his flagship Homestead, and on the other side the battle-scarred leviathans Duquesne and Edgar Thomson which, twenty years ago, defeated the proud champions of Great Britain and established American supremacy. One of the vessels is forty-three years old; but every one of them is fighting class trim. There are no hulks, no slow or unworthy craft, and there are forty-five thousand men behind the guns. The payroll of this fleet is fifteen million a year. It is practically thirty fleets under one control. On the deck of the Edgar Thomson is a tiny figure, which can scarcely be distinguished with a strong field glass. That little man, you are told, is Andrew Carnegie, owner of the fleet."[7]

In ten years Edgar Thomson Works had changed the face of the world steel market. It had surpassed the great works of Germany and Britain. Steel makers from all over the world were coming to Braddock to see and learn. It was the training ground for future steel and American industry management. It gave America a cost system that could be integrated into managerial and operational practices. Edgar Thomson Works operating design was the basis of continuous throughput and Just-In-Time programs throughout the world. Edgar Thomson Works became the birthplace of industrial chemistry and ferrous metallurgy. It produced over 30 millionaires but its real gift to industry was a group of leaders known as "the Boys of Braddock," who would change the face of industry forever.

---

[7] Casson, 216

Chapter 6

> "Take away all our money, our great works, ore mines and coke ovens but leave our organization and in four years I shall have re-established myself."
>
> —*Andrew Carnegie*

Captain Bill Jones

The real story of Braddock's Edgar Thomson plant was the men. Under the guidance of an almost mythical manager, Captain Bill Jones, Carnegie would get an empire and America would get world manufacturing leadership. It would be a great mistake to attribute this to Carnegie's capital and investment. Carnegie first built his financial base using a group of "young geniuses" of his boyhood days. Carnegie then built his industrial empire on another group of young geniuses known as the 'boys of Braddock." In Jones's obituary it was said: "He was Captain of Industry, unsurpassed as an organizer, marvelous in his knowledge of detail, fertile in expedients and invention; always planning new victories and winning them."

Of the pioneers of the Bessemer process, Jones was the one who brought the human element to bear. Historian Casson said, "Kelly lived in the world of ideas; Ward, in a world of money; Holley, in a world of scientific knowledge; and Jones in the world of men." Jones was the man on whom Carnegie built his company, and Jones trained the managers on whom United States Steel and Bethlehem Steel would be built. The real contribution of Jones would be a spirit and philosophy that would cause a revolution in industry via a group of followers known as the "boys of Braddock." Carnegie's own statement stands as testimony: "So perfect was the machinery, so admirable the plans, so skillful were the men selected by Captain Jones, and so great a manager was he himself, that our success was phenomenal."[1] Bill Jones's spirit would carry Carnegie Steel and United States Steel Corporation for over hundred years via the army of managers Jones developed. Carnegie so admired him that he had a portrait of him in all his homes and offices.

In 1873, as Edgar Thomson Works was about to start, the Cambria Iron Company was involved in a major labor dispute. Carnegie conceived the idea to try to get some of the best Bessemer steel men in the country. Carnegie found success gaining Captain William Jones for his plant superintendent. A key group of Cambria managers followed: Captain Lapsley, superintendent of the rail mill; John Rinard, superintendent of the converting works; Thomas James, superintendent of machinery; F. Bridges, superintendent of transportation and Thomas Addenbrook, head furnace builder were but a few. The exodus was not just managers but rollers such as Andrew Boyle, furnace men and handlers. This gave the new works an expert workforce to start with and the best Bessemer steel management group in the world.

The early success of the plant was attributed to these men by an 1875 publication of *American Manufacturer* magazine: "successful operation is greatly do to the large experience in Bessemer manufacture of Capt. William R. Jones, general superintendent of the works and of Capt. Thomas H. Lapsley, superintendent of the rolling mill."

The physical and spiritual roots of Edgar Thomson Works must therefore be found in Johnstown and the Cambria Iron Company. It was at Cambria that Bill Jones came to the forefront. We have already seen some of the history of this great Johnstown mill. It, however, is the men of Cambria we need to focus on now. Carnegie early in his career said, "The

---

[1] Carnegie, 196

Cambria Works have produced more great steel makers than any other works in the United States."[2] The father of the Cambria plant was Daniel Morrell. Morrell is a difficult man to fully understand. He had moments of brilliance, moments of hard-headed backward thinking, at times a straight shooter with his employees and at other times working behind their backs: characteristics which probably helped him later in life, when he was elected to Congress. Morrell was a Quaker from Philadelphia with a financial background. He was sent by Philadelphia bankers and stockholders to aid the floundering Cambria Iron Works in the 1850s. He was also a partner of Captain Ward's Detroit Kelly process rail mill, which failed prior to the Civil War. While having a banking background, Morrell loved science and metallurgy. He shortly became a knowledgeable metallurgist and iron master. In the 1870s, he refused to partner with Carnegie, who Morrell thought was merely a bonds salesman not an iron master.

Morrell, however, was the right man for Carnegie to borrow from. Morrell was much like Carnegie in his approach to management. Morrell, the "Quaker Ironmaster," had a deep belief that the best equipment and people must be brought to bear in successful operations. He brought Kelly to Cambria to experiment with pneumatic steel making in the 1850s. In the 1860s, he brought Holley to build a Bessemer converting plant at Johnstown. Morrell would also bring the best rolling mill engineers to Cambria in John and George Fritz. Morrell also was committed to using only American labor. Most Bessemer mills were bringing in English laborers and engineers. Morrell choose to train Americans. To that end, Morrell built a library and a night school for his employees to learn science, mechanical drawing and engineering. Morrell was a believer in training American youth for the mills as well. Morrell and later Carnegie were instrumental in requiring mechanical and

---

[2] Casson, 19

work training in Pennsylvania grade schools. In my grade schools in the early nineteen sixties, it was still Pennsylvania law that seventh and eighth graders take mechanical drawing. Morrell was also the first to build an industrial hospital for the steelworks.

Morrell was a people person. He owned one of the few mills that did not enforce the brutal twelve-hour day. Morrell believed productivity and ethics were best met by the eight-hour day. His young manager at Cambria, Bill Jones, learned and later made it a cornerstone of his own philosophy. In a famous speech later in Congress, Morrell noted, "The American workingman must live in a house, not a hut; he must wear decent clothes and eat wholesome and nourishing food. He is an integral part of the municipality, the State, and the nation; subject to no fetters of class or caste; neither pauper, nor peasant, nor serf, but a free American citizen." Certainly no union president could have defended the American workingman better. So how did labor trouble come to Cambria?

Morrell's blind side was the rise of unions in the steel industry. His behavior towards the worker was an enigma. On one hand he was progressive and giving, on the other it was take it or leave it. At heart Morrell was a product of his times. He was above all an Industrial Victorian, who distrusted foreigners. Hungarians in particular had come in great numbers to the mines in the surrounding hills and to the Johnstown mill of Cambria. Morrell deemed Johnstown a company town and labor unions were not welcome. Johnstown was the definition of a company town with its company department store and 700 company houses, which were rented to the workers. Morrell took care of the workers but demanded complete loyalty and tolerated nothing less. Company rule number 9 prohibited any secret associations or unions among his employees. Still, on the management side, Morrell was a finder and developer of great engineers.

What Morrell failed to realize was that it was not engineering alone that produced steel. Managers were needed. Morrell focused on his managers having outstanding technical skills. A man like Bill Jones was difficult for Morrell to understand.

One of the first of the engineers Morrell developed was John Fritz. Ultimately the American steel industry would call Fritz the "Dean of Steel makers." John and his brother George were the greatest of the Bessemer rolling mill engineers. In 1857 they invented the first three-high rail rolling mills at Cambria. This invention was a major improvement in the productivity of rolling mills. John would move on in the early 1860s to re-build a small iron works in Bethlehem, Pennsylvania into the Bethlehem Steel Corporation. George would stay and would continue the world-class rolling operation at Cambria. Jones added rolling expertise to his furnace knowledge by working with the Fritz brothers at Cambria.

The greatest manager to come to Cambria was Captain Bill Jones. Morrell had brought Jones to Cambria and moved him up based on his engineering talents, missing Jones's real strength as a leader and manager. When I teach operations and manufacturing management at the University, Bill Jones is my classic model for a manager. Bill Jones was a "franchise player." Bill Jones was the man who built Carnegie steel. Bill Jones was a manager who actually protected his men better than the union. Jones's story deserves some space.

Jones was born on February 23, 1830 to a Welsh family in Catasauqua, Pennsylvania. Catasauqua was the home of Crane Iron Works. At age ten, Bill Jones started working at Crane Iron. The manager of Crane, David Thomas, was one of the best charcoal furnace men in the business. Thomas was an innovator and risk taker. Under Thomas, Crane Iron was one of the first to replace charcoal with anthracite coal. He also was the first iron works to use a hot air blast in the blast furnace, which caused major increases in furnace output. A young Jones was indeed blessed to learn from the expertise of Thomas. Jones developed into a furnace expert as well, eventually moving for a short period to Cambria Iron in Johnstown.

His reputation got him a promotion to build a furnace in Chattanooga, Tennessee. Jones was a short muscular man with a slight speech impediment. It was his spirit that destined him to leadership. With the Civil War, he enlisted in the Union army. As a corporal he distinguished himself at the battles of Fredericksburg and Chancellorsville. In the Gettysburg campaign he was promoted to captain. He was a natural, caring leader. He was extremely proud of his Civil War service. He would later in life donate a memorial at the Braddock cemetery to the Grand Army of the Republic.

After the Civil War, he returned to the Cambria Iron Company. At Cambria, Jones worked with Alexander Holley in the conversion of the plant to the Bessemer process. Jones was a knowledgeable and experienced furnace engineer. Jones rose to plant superintendent at Cambria under George Fritz, who was General Superintendent based on his technical skills. George Fritz was considered the best rolling mill man in the world. Again as an understudy to Fritz, Jones improved his rolling expertise. Jones was an outstanding mechanic. He was a great innovator. The real legacy of Jones was, however, his management skills. The leadership during combat that Jones had shown continued as an operating manager. He had those rare characteristics that allowed for toughness and kindness in the same stroke. He was able to blend corporate goals with the personal goals of his men, generating one accomplishment after another. Some of this was his love of sports that made him a record keeper and breaker. The men who worked for him demonstrated extreme loyalty.

His philosophy as a manager was certainly affected by his Cambria experience with Morrell. The following is an example of Bill Jones's managerial beliefs in his own words: "The men should be made to feel that the company is interested in their welfare. Make the works a pleasant place for them. I have always found it best to treat men well, and I find that my men are anxious to retain my good will by working steadily and honestly, and instead of dodging are anxious to show me what a good day's work they have done. All haughty and disdainful treatment of men has a very decided and bad effect on them." Bill Jones was always able to motivate men even with his hot temper.

Jones lived by his words. He was known to give money out of his pocket to help working families. When as a manager at Johnstown and Braddock, his men achieved a new record, he would take them to a Pittsburgh baseball game. Jones never achieved the wealth of Carnegie but on a percent basis out-gave Carnegie. He was always helping out his workers and their families. Probably the greatest tribute to his generosity was at his funeral in Braddock. The *Pittsburgh Gazette* reported that 10,000 tearful residents of Braddock lined the streets of his funeral procession. Reading the accounts of that funeral still amazes me. I have never heard of any manager having anywhere near this level of attendance at a funeral.

Jones had fought against the whole steel industry demanding an eight-hour day over the industry standard of twelve hours. He believed the twelve-hour day to be not only brutal but counter-productive. He believed the motivated men working eight hours could out-perform the physically and mentally worn down men of a twelve-hour shift. The core of his belief was productivity as the goal. He challenged his men often for higher production with steak dinners. He had a passion for achieving goals and breaking records. This type of personal achievement took priority over money. While he commanded a huge salary, he gave most of it away motivating his men and helping the community. These types of leaders are rare.

He loved baseball, horse racing and gambling as well. These fun-loving events were his only outlet from long days in the mill. These personal preferences put him in poor standing with his Quaker owner, Morrell. One historian noted, "Morrell, his Quaker employer, would have discharged him if it had not been for the undeniable fact that Jones could get more work out of a gang of men than any other boss in the iron business."[3] His friendship with the men made him also to appear soft on labor as Cambria moved into its 1870s struggles. Morrell believed that Jones's strength had become his weakness. This time, however, Morrell was off base. Jones's love of sports was only another facet of his achievement-oriented personality. It was the secret of his ability to get more work than any other manager out of a group of men. Another managerial approach that Morrell could not understand was his love and care of the foreign "bohunks" and "hunkies." Jones as a manager learned to value men for their accomplishments, not nationality. He was a friend and supporter of the Hungarian furnace laborers, the lowest paid in the mill. This was a learned value since in his boyhood in a very poor mill town; he was part of gang that found fun in throwing stones at the immigrant Irish kids.

Morrell had really missed the point of Bill Jones as a friend of labor. It was that very friendship that motivated men to achieve unheard-of records. In the *American Manufacturer* magazine the following was said on Jones's death: "No one more honestly and with more singleness of purpose strove in every way to help and benefit those under him than Captain

---

[3] Casson, 23

Jones. Himself from the ranks of labor, he never forgot the fact and looked at all questions affecting the relations of employer and employed in the works he managed from the standpoint of both of these relations; and both employer and employed have come to realize that his judgment was in the main wise as they have always believed it was honest." Morrell and Jones remained at odds for most of his career at Cambria.

The final break with Morrell came when George Fritz died. Fritz had been General Superintendent of Cambria. Morrell promoted another man over Bill Jones. Morrell felt that Jones was too weak on managing! Jones did have a huge ego and that was a blow he could not accept. It was a resentment that he would use to pole-vault his new plant, Edgar Thomson Works, over Morrell's Cambria. On hearing of Morrell's passing him over, Jones said, "As for me, I'm going to straighten up, go somewhere else, and show them what I can do." Morrell found out that Bill Jones was not a man you wanted to give resentment to. Jones as Superintendent of Edgar Thomson Works would initially target every known Cambria steel making record to take down. Jones got great happiness in taking each record away from Cambria. In a year, Edgar Thomson Works was out-performing Cambria Iron in every department. The following is from a letter from Carnegie while on tour in Italy in 1878 referring the breaking of some Cambria Iron Company records: "Pyramids & Mt. Etna & Vesuvius have been our last climbs-Mt E of course we did only the base, tell Capt Jones there was a proud little stout man who gave a wild hurrah when he saw E T ahead. Wasn't it a close race with Cambria Iron Company but they had a start, besides we had to go through the measles you know." It can be said that it was a single resentment that took Edgar Thomson Works to the best in the world.

Jones was the man Carnegie wanted to manage Edgar Thomson Works for many reasons. First, he recognized his leadership skills. This is where Morrell and Carnegie differed. Carnegie put people first while for Morrell it was technology. Second, Carnegie knew he was a brilliant engineer who had worked with Holley to set up Cambria's Bessemer plant. Jones would therefore be an excellent complement as construction manager to Holley as the designer. Third, Carnegie cared only in results, not managerial styles or theories. Last, bringing Jones over to Edgar Thomson Works would bring in a large following from Cambria. Of course these are but a few of the major reasons. Carnegie as a businessman knew that by bringing in Jones, he would be able to fully analyze Cambria as a competitor. While Jones believed in excellent treatment of the worker, he did not necessarily believe in high wages, concept Carnegie liked. Jones believed probably to a fault that all men worked for achievement. Jones based this assumption on his own tendencies. Carnegie moved quickly to hire Bill Jones because he saw himself in Jones.

Bill Jones, like Carnegie, was a community man. He was well known and could often be seen eating peanuts and smoking cigars on the streets of Braddock. Jones was loved by many and was always willing to employ the sons of his workers. He loved horseracing and set up a racetrack in Braddock. He was an early stockholder in the Pittsburgh baseball club (Duquesne Grays), which he loved. After the great Johnstown Flood, Jones organized Braddock volunteers to help in disaster relief. His flood relief at Johnstown showed his generosity and humility. One writer noted: "Jones had paid out of his own pocket for supplies he had brought to Johnstown and the wages of the men he had taken with him. In an interview with the Pittsburgh Press he gave great credit to the leadership Moxham had shown and added that he had a hundred or so Hungarians working for him and that they worked like horses."[4] The *Pittsburgh Gazette* in 1889 estimated that Jones gave $10,000 a year to charity alone based on a $50,000 per year salary as manager of Edgar Thomson Works. He was known to donate to the churches of all denominations. When a local pastor, Reverend C. DeLong, came to Jones to build a Sunday school, Jones supplied the works carpenters to build the building and got Carnegie to donate the books.

Jones would also be a developer of generations of steel managers. Jones more than Carnegie was the heart and soul of Carnegie Steel. Like Carnegie, Jones could mold men and teach them. Jones's Boys or what one historian called the "boys of Braddock" would transform American industry. One of those boys Jones found and groomed was Charles Schwab. Schwab later noted one of Jones's superstitions while working at Edgar Thomson was the need for all to work on New Year's Day. Schwab recalled: "On one New Year's Day I was sick in bed. Along in the morning a wagon drew up to the house. New drawings for the mill had to be started. Jones had taken a cart, loaded it with some of the office furnishings, including my drawing board, and had brought it home to me, so that I could get to work, New Year's Day, on the new rail mill."

Besides his drives, loves and generosity, Jones was a man of pride. He had a fierce temper. He was known to fire a man, only to come back after an hour to sign him up again. Still many tried hard to avoid his famous temper. Even Carnegie treaded lightly. The classic story of his ego was when he was going to make him a partner with the usual stock holding. Jones held out for the salary of the President of the United States ($25,000), which Carnegie happily paid. It was not just ego; Jones also worried that being a partner would put distance between him and the men.

---

[4] McCullough, 229

Jones was also the ideal match for the new cost accounting system of Shinn and Carnegie, which focused on cost per ton. Jones established a policy to utilize the better-cost analysis and bring down cost per ton. It became known as the "scrap heap" policy. The "scrap policy" meant that new investment would be favored to reduce cost per ton. That meant that no matter how new the equipment, it would be scrapped quickly if newer equipment offered a reduction in cost per ton costs. It is in fact a bold operating policy. It creates the proper balance needed to increase productivity. It gives the men the right equipment with which to excel. Very few operating managers understand this balance. Jones talked of harmony between men, equipment, production, quality and safety. To that purpose Jones paid attention to things like shop ventilation that affected the comfort and safety of the workers. Jones believed that if you pushed production over safety in the short run, the long run result was a lost of productivity. Jones was a real pioneer in safety. The Pittsburgh steel industry in the 1880s was deadly, to put it lightly. Historian Peter Krass described it: "the introduction of faster moving equipment and machinery contributed to the increase in accidents. Fatal accidents in the steel industry accounted for 20% of the total adult male mortality in Pittsburgh; among the 'ignorant' southern and eastern European immigrants the rate shot to 40%. Pittsburgh had one of the highest accident rates of all U.S. cities, and the *National Labor Tribune* asserted there were as many unreported deaths and injuries as there were reported. Sadly, the newspaper observed the list of killed and wounded in a given year was as long as a small battle in the Civil War."[5] Jones realized that safety and production were interrelated. Jones was one of the earliest to see the relationship between working conditions and productivity. His belief and demonstration of that factor in productivity would

---

[5] Krass, 218

help later management experts such as the famous Frederick Taylor.

A number of Bill Jones-trained "boys of Braddock" would go out into industry and develop world-class safety programs in America. Some years later, Frederick Taylor, the "father of Scientific Management" would confirm Jones's views in several major studies. In 1911 Taylor reported to Congress a three-year study finding that the steel mills with the highest productivity also had the best safety record. Another of the boys, William Dickson, would also be affected by the Jones philosophy and would change safety practices in American industry.

Under Jones the works was constantly being upgraded. Within a few years Jones upgraded from two five-ton converters to two seven-ton converters. In 1882 Jones moved to three ten-ton converters so Edgar Thomson Works could stay ahead of shops at Bethlehem, Steelton and Chicago. Jones's objective always was to be first in production and productivity. For forty years Edgar Thomson works would remain untouched in production output and productivity.

Another part of the Jones improvement was innovation. Probably Jones's most famous patent was the "Jones Mixer." This mixer was a large storage and mixing vessel that took molten pig iron from several different blast furnaces. This invention allowed for a continuous and uniform flow of liquid pig iron to the Bessemer converters. The Jones mixer coupled with the Holley Bessemer quick-change trunnion allowed for truly continuous hot steel production. Another forward thinking innovation was the use of steel bolts in rail mill housings. Rail mills by nature took a constant pounding and high impacts from the rolling of steel. Wrought iron bolts didn't have the strength or quality. Jones replaced them with steel. Amazingly recent studies of the sinking of the *Titanic* suggest that steel bolts might have sparred it. The *Titanic* was one of the earliest Bessemer steel ships but the bolts remained the lower-strength wrought iron. The stress of the iceberg may have exceeded the strength of wrought iron. This is exactly what was happening on the rolling mills: bolts were being sheared off. Interestingly, Jones was a big believer in large design safety factors. Jones reported the following to the British Iron and Steel Institute in 1882: "In all new machinery the aim is to get an excess of strength; the usual factor of safety in new rolling machinery is not allowable. The machinery must be extra heavy and strong, so the inertia of the mass will swallow all strains thrown upon it."

Still always at the heart of Jones's philosophy was that men want to achieve and love to break records. The motivation was more basic than money. In fact Jones was convinced that it was success, pride, power and achievement that were the real motivators. Jones hired men who would fit this philosophy building an organization of over-achievers. It was a highly competitive environment that reinforced the philosophy. It was an environment where ambition and drive could take a common laborer to manager in a few years. These types of success stories further reinforced the philosophy. Combining this type of working environment with the best equipment in the world as at Edgar Thomson Works would create industrial history.

In 1875, just before Edgar Thomson Works was to open, Jones laid out in a letter to Carnegie partner, McCandless, what would be needed for success. The letter centered on three points:

> 1. *"We must be careful of the class of men we collect."*
> Jones believed as always the men where the core of success. He was in line with Morrell, Fritz and Holley on the use of Native Americans. He went on to say, "My experience has shown that Germans and Irish, Swedes and what I denominate "Buckwheats" — young

American country boys — judiciously mixed, make the most effective and tractable force you can find." Later as Hungarians and Southern Europeans came to the mill, Jones was one of the first to include them in bonus systems. Jones believed strongly that it was not the nationality that was important but the attitude. Jones wanted men who loved achievement and competition like him. Edgar Thomson Works under Jones was a mass of over-achieving competitors at all levels.

2. *"It should be the aim of the firm to keep the works running steadily."* This was a somewhat different theory of Jones's. He believed low wages could be paid if work was kept steady. Again he thought the steady low wages paid better than up and down high wages cut off by production stops and strikes. It's a theory that volume washes out all evils. It was popularized in the steel industry for years by Jones's success with it.

3. *"The company should endeavor to make the cost of living as low as possible."* This again is part of his theory to make low wages work. Jones had seen the use of company housing and company stores at Cambria. Jones worked with Carnegie to help the men get low cost loans for houses. Jones got Carnegie to build a cooperative store for cheaper dry goods as well as food. Sons of the steelworkers were given jobs to build family income.

It was a theory not always in step with Carnegie's thinking but Carnegie always yielded to the results of Bill Jones. In fairness, Jones's managerial techniques required a dynamic manager to be successful and it was not for everybody. Still, many great men, such as Charles Schwab, would learn from Jones to successfully apply these methods and management techniques.

Jones hated unions and felt that company support for needs such as housing was a better option than higher wages. He had seen this type of support work at Johnstown, where Morrell supplied company housing. In the midst of great labor struggles across river at Homestead in 1882, Jones suggested the following to Carnegie: "I think our men are now getting to be satisfied, and I see signs of the old Esprit De Corps. I am going slow and carefully. I now feel sure that the Union will not get a foothold here. I will ask the Company to agree to loan such good men as I may select say from 60—$800 this year to assist them in the building homes. This is an effective plan to keep out the Union. Every good man that wants to build, encourage. You should calculate on a reasonable investment in that direction. Give them the money on fair interest."[6]

One of Jones's apparent failures at the Works was the eight-hour working day he believed so strongly in. That apparent defeat would some years later be forged into a national working standard. It was a belief that had formed by his experience with Morrell and Cambria Works. The twelve-hour turn included a twenty-four-rotation shift, the so-called "long turn" every two weeks. One writer described the long turn as: "The barbaric long turn, or twenty-four hour shift, was the means by which workmen rotated from the night shift back to the day shift and back. A day shift worker for example, would labor from six o'clock Sunday morning and around the clock to six o'clock Monday morning. Then, after twelve hours off, he would report for work at six on Monday evening and every evening thereafter for the next two weeks."[7] Jones early on had started Edgar Thomson Works on the eight-hour shift and was setting new productivity records daily.

---

[6] Krass, 179

[7] Gerald G. Eggert, *Steelmasters and Labor Reform, 1886-1923* (Pittsburgh: University of Pittsburgh Press, 1981), 8

Carnegie continued to pressure Jones to use the twelve-hour day at Edgar Thomson using accounting data to make his case. That fact was that Jones's eight-hour schedule had been more productive and was paying for itself. Carnegie continued to tolerate the Jones methodology because production records fell weekly. The pressure increased as Coke King, Henry Clay Frick became a partner with the Carnegie brothers. Frick had no understanding or respect for the workingman. Frick saw workers as cost streams in the production process. A prelude to the great Homestead strike was developing at Edgar Thomson Works. In December of 1887, Edgar Thomson Works was closed for refurbishing and rebuilding. The winter shutdown put 2000 men out of work.[8] Carnegie realized the lack of wages during the shutdown added the needed leverage to propose a new sliding pay scale, overall ten percent pay cut and a return to the twelve-hour day.

The fledgling union, the Knights of Labor, objected to Carnegie's proposal, calling for a strike. Since the plant was already shut down, a strike initially had little impact. Carnegie had in 1885 had already forced the Amalgamated Union out of Edgar Thomson by forcing all workers to sign a contract renouncing the union, known as "yellow dog" contracts. The Amalgamated union with its lodges clearly threatened the paternal managerial system that had been so successful at Edgar Thomson Works. The Knights of Labor had the strong support of the lowest paid employees such as the Slavs and Hungarians. Carnegie was still reeling from a strike at his newly obtained Frick Coke, which caused a major reduction of pig iron at Braddock. The Knights of Labor was made up of a mix of skilled and unskilled labor. Carnegie believed this mix of skilled and unskilled workers was the Knights' Achilles' heel. Carnegie stated the following to a reporter on the Knights of Labor: "It is one of those ephemeral organizations

---

[8] Krass, 223

that go up like a rocket and come down like a stick. It is founded upon false principles, viz., that they could combine common or unskilled labor with skilled." Still the Knights had the support of the high paid Irish furnace workers and the Welsh in the rolling mills.

Carnegie was able to avert some of the labor trouble at Edgar Thomson Works by straightforward talk and negotiations with the men. Carnegie discussed one of these in his *Autobiography;* the dispute was over the pay scale at Edgar Thomson Works. The men had made an agreement but wanted to change it four months before the agreement expired. Carnegie asked Bill Jones to set three committees to represent the men and bring them to New York. In the discussion Carnegie won the argument that the agreement was to be stood by to the expiration. Carnegie was straightforward: "You may leave the blast furnaces. The grass will grow around them before we yield to your threat. The worst day that labor has ever seen in this world is that day in which it dishonors itself by breaking its agreement. You have your answer."

Jones was caught in the middle of this struggle but in the end he stood with Carnegie. The men were willing to accept the wage changes but refused to return to a twelve-hour day. Carnegie and Frick hired Pinkerton guards and started to hire new non-union employees. Several workers were killed in the struggles at the plant gates. Ultimately the Knights of Labor did not have the solidarity to maintain the strike. The large population of new mill immigrant workers needed to eat and the "strike" ended in May of 1888. This struggle would augur the deaths of the Homestead strike in 1892, where the Knights of Labor would remember the Braddock defeat. With it came an end to the eight-hour day at Edgar Thomson Works. It was a discouraging setback to Bill Jones. Jones's younger managers, the "boys of Braddock," would later lead American management back to it in the 1930s but it would be a long struggle. In a hearing before Congress, long after Jones's death, his eight-hour day at the Braddock works would be remembered and immortalized.

Jones's one concession to the philosophy of the Industrial Victorians was his hatred of unions. Jones believed unions broke individual motivation. He believed that management should treat people right. Treating people right would negate the need for unions. He was always an advocate of labor but never a supporter of the unions. In particular, he hated the Amalgamated Association of Iron and Steel workers, which represented the better jobs, particularly in the Irish controlled furnaces. The Knights of Labor representing the low paying immigrant jobs, he seemed to tolerate to some degree. This view may seem inconsistent with he love of the worker but Jones assumed managerial fair treatment. Fair treatment of the mill "hunkies" was rare among the managers of his day. Jones did allow an informal system of control by nationalities, which favored the Irish, Welsh and Germans in the skilled positions. Many biographers of Carnegie noted that the skilled workers of Braddock lived a good life. One of these biographers, Bernard Alderson, quoted Carnegie: "The lot of a skilled workman is far better than that of the heir to an hereditary title." For the most part Jones was in agreement with Carnegie.

Jones, however, was opposed to Carnegie's return to the twelve-hour day. Jones was one a few who was not afraid to take on Carnegie. Still Carnegie won this one. Jones was upset with the emerging union, the Knights of Labor, for its focus on pay scales versus working conditions. In 1888, Jones was quoted in the *National Labor Tribune*: "I charge the Knights of Labor with gross dereliction of duty when after establishing as a general rule the eight-hour day... made no effort to take it to other establishments."[9] The real fact of the matter is that an

---

[9] Fitch, 116

eight-hour day would not only increase employment but also reduce worker take-home pay. At the time the union was more interested in preventing the market price sliding wage scale as well as assuring the union's right to organize.

Jones was not an Industrial Victorian like Carnegie and Frick in any of his operating approaches. His progressive style in managing coupled with his economic conservatism really can be used to classify an evolving group of managers: the Industrial Edwardians. While Jones was a mechanic and natural engineer, he showed no interest in science. Jones believed the chemistry was not needed because a furnace man could achieve the same end product with his eyes. Jones said, "Chemistry will be the god damn ruin of this industry." Jones was rare in that he had the experience to make molten steel by feel alone. Jones was a master of furnaces. From 1875 to 1882, as plant manager, Jones brought in 4 blast furnaces. Each of these blast furnaces set world output records and low coke consumption records as well. The blast furnaces of Edgar Thomson were unequaled in the world market. By 1877, only few years after opening, the blast furnaces, Bessemer converters and blooming mill combination was producing more steel than could be rolled at the rail mill. The Carnegie partners proceeded to find new applications such as springs, axles and plowshares. These products had been dominated by the higher quality crucible steel. This broke one of the still lingering myths of Carnegie Steel that production came first.

Most people still attribute Carnegie Steel successes to production. Certainly the production records of Edgar Thomson Works had amazed the world. Quality, however, was what captured the huge Bessemer steel market and expanded it into other areas. In 1880 Carnegie looked back at Edgar Thomson Works's initial success and said, "I have never known a concern to make a decided success that did not do good, honest work, and even in these days of fiercest competition, when everything would seem to be a matter of price, there lies still at the root of great business success the very much more important factor of quality. The effect of attention to quality cannot be overestimated."

In May 1881, Jones presented a paper to the British Iron and Steel Institute on the success of Edgar Thomson Works. These are some of the key points of that paper:

1. *"While we of Edgar Thomson were compelled (being engaged in erecting the works) to listen to their wonderful stories."* Bill Jones is referring here to the records being set at Cambria, Steelton and Joliet. Jones loved benchmarking records. Edgar Thomson was built to compete! World records were followed and published. Bill Jones was way ahead of most of American industry; it has only been in the last thirty years that benchmarking has come into vogue. Jones posted records in the mills from all over the industry and world as goals for the crews. Record breaking was a passion if not an obsession.

2. *"Esprit de corps"* Jones the sports lover modeled his managerial approach similarly. He believed in teamwork and noted it as the root to Edgar Thomson Works's success. Jones further stated, *"As long as the record made by the works stands the first so long are they content to labor at a moderate rate; but let it be known that some rival establishment has beaten that record, and then there is no content until the rival's record is eclipsed."* This was a powerful technique of Jones and it assured competitive advantage. Through Jones's letters and writing to Carnegie you see a focus on morale.

3. *"The diversity of nationality of the workmen."* Jones believed that mixed nationalities was part of the success. Jones described the make out of his crews as:

"Representatives from England, Ireland, Scotland, Wales, and all parts of Germany, Swedes, Hungarians, and a few French and Italians, with a small percent of coloured workmen." He believed the multiple nationalities brought strength to an organization but he favored the group he called, "'Buckwheats' — young American country boys." His paper was politically correct for the audience since he included the English in a long list of nationalities. Jones like his former Cambria boss, Morrell, disliked the English. On English workmen he once told a Carnegie partner that, "but mark me, Englishmen have been the worst class of men I have had anything to do with." While Jones supported diversity, Edgar Thomson Works was segmented in "lodges." The Irish controlled the high paying furnace jobs; the Welsh and Germans controlled the high paying rolling mill jobs, while the Hungarians and Slavs had the low paying labor jobs. Still Jones protected these low paying jobs and better working conditions.

4. *"Facilities for getting the ingots out of the road."* Jones's objective was world-class production and productivity. Jones combined benchmarking; the scrap heap policy and innovation to assure that Edgar Thomson Works could out produce any competitor. Jones realized that Carnegie could sell anything he could produce. Speed of throughput was another key to the Jones's operating philosophy. Continuous flow was a hallmark of the Jones system. This emphasis led Jones to develop preventive maintenance systems to avoid the stoppage of production.

5. *"In increasing the output of these works, I soon discovered it was entirely out of the question to expect human flesh and blood to labor incessantly for twelve hours, and therefore it was decided to put on three*

turns, reducing the hours of labor to eight." Jones was the eight-hour day's biggest supporter. He was alone on this point against the Industrial Victorians of the day. Carnegie allowed it at Edgar Thomson Works because of Jones but ran most of Carnegie Steel on the twelve-hour, seven-day system. Jones, however, inspired some of the "boys of Braddock" who would later change the standard for American industry.

6. *"Another important matter connected with fast working is maintenance of machinery."* Here again Jones was way ahead of his time. Most of the Industrial Victorians, as today, were addicted to breakdown maintenance. That breakdown philosophy merely ran things until they broke and then sent in the repair crew. Jones's passion for production records gave him an abnormal fear of a work stoppage. Jones was the father of preventive maintenance. Holley and Jones had also pioneered the use of quick change out of "tooling." In this case the tooling was the Bessemer brick lined vessel. They designed a trunnion (ring) system to allow a worn-out vessel to be quickly changed without interfering with production.

Edgar Thomson remained king of the hill but not without several challenges.

The end for Bill Jones came by surprise for Edgar Thomson Works. On the night of September 6, 1889, furnace "C" had a major problem. It was known as hanging, which blocked the production of pig iron because material was stuck in the furnace stack. With him that night were many of the "boys of Braddock" such as Charles Schwab, David Kerr and James Gayley. Jones was first in trying to get things moving. Suddenly the furnace busted, knocking Jones down. He was knocked unconscious by the fall. He was taken to the Pittsburgh Homeopathic Hospital and Carnegie rushed in his personal doctor. On September 28, 1889, having never gained consciousness, Bill Jones died. He left his wife (an invalid) and two children. Jones, however, would be remembered. For decades people would be talking of having had worked with the great Captain Jones.

In reality, Jones left a spirit that would be part of Edgar Thomson Works and Carnegie Steel. Like the battle of Braddock, Jones left a mark on the town and the company. Jones's "boys" would go on to dominate the Carnegie Company, the steel industry and American industry. Several of his staff such as Charles Schwab, Alva Dinkey and James Gayley would be future top executives in the steel and American industry. Hundreds of his men would raise to managerial positions not only in the future United States Steel but American industry as a whole. Jones's Blast Furnace manager, Julian Kennedy, became the world expert in furnace design, and as a consultant to J. P. Morgan was a creator of United States Steel. James Gayley would rise to become vice-president of United States Steel. Many of his managerial techniques would start a revolution in American manufacturing. James Gayley summarized Jones's career: "You can say that Captain Jones, through his mechanical contributions did fully as much as Mushet or Sir Henry Bessemer." The spirit of Captain Bill may never have left Braddock over the years. Again and again Edgar Thomson Works would stand for moderation in the unionization struggle over the next fifty years. Somehow against the odds only Edgar Thomson Works has survived the downfall of steel in the Monongahela valley.

Bill Jones had demonstrated that a union was not needed if management would behave properly. The inability of the union to sign employees at Edgar Thomson Works was related to a number of factors during his administration. First, the men trusted Bill Jones and his assistant, Charles Schwab. Bill Jones filled the role of union president between the men and Carnegie. Jones had demonstrated that he was interested in the overworked conditions of the workers. The workers' trust was so deep that they even allowed Carnegie's sliding scale to be implemented. They believed that Jones would battle Carnegie and get it changed.

Secondly the Jones administration informally allowed the nationality leaders to control employment and to some degree wages. For example an Irish immigrant would go to one of these "leaders" who would get him a job in the mill. Some of these informal leaders were actually leaders in the secret union lodges. It was in effect an informal union. The Irish had a tradition of secret union membership going back to the "Molly Maguires" in north-central Ireland.

Thirdly the Amalgamated union across the board equal representation threatened the higher paying jobs of the Braddock "natives," the Irish, Welsh and Scottish. This was popular cultural racism to hold the Hungarians and Slavs down. The union threatened the lodge system that favored the higher paying jobs and nationalities.

Lastly the union never really caught on with the higher paid employees. In general Jones treatment offered a better alternative being fair and balanced.

Jones had clearly shown his skill in organizational management. The "boys of Braddock" would immortalize Jones in the spread of his management beliefs. The Jones managerial line would dominate American management for the next forty years. The eight-hour day would come to the industry in the 1920s. Jones's management techniques like benchmarking, production bonuses, improved safety, better working conditions and improved cost of living would become the core of American management principles. There has been no better practitioner of managing than Bill Jones. Jones showed the magic of bringing workers, managers and equipment together (harmony). Carnegie knew he that it was Bill Jones who was responsible for his empire. Carnegie would have a painting of Bill Jones in his New York mansion bedroom until his death.

Jones's mark on American industry is still being felt today. Respect for the workingman, promotion from within and from the ranks and the eight-hour day were cornerstones of his labor policy. Preventive maintenance programs and inventions like the Jones mixer assured continuous steel making. Jones had invented the concept of integrated process control with his idea of working harmony. His real legacy, however, was the long line of managers such as Charles Schwab groomed by Jones.

CHAPTER 7

"He was a great general. He had a true sense of proportion, an appreciation of the relative value of conflicting factors, a mind that could grasp the most complex situation, and last, but not least, he inspired his men with confidence in him and his ability, had perfect knowledge of human nature, and absolute mastery of men."
—*William Brennan*

CHARLES SCHWAB: THE STEEL TITAN

Charles Schwab was the managerial creation of Bill Jones. Schwab was a product of the emerging steel town of Braddock and Edgar Thomson Works. He was the first of a group of steel makers to be dubbed by the press as the "boys of Braddock." Going to Braddock to start a steel career was like an artist going to Carnegie Hall in New York. Jones had honed Schwab into a master manager. In the end, however, Schwab would go places that Jones could not have. Schwab was a polished Bill Jones. Schwab always attributed his success to training under Bill Jones. Schwab would later recall: "I had over me an impetuous, hustling man. It was necessary for me to be up to the top notch to give satisfaction. I worked faster than I otherwise would have done, and to him I attribute the impetus that I acquired. My whole object in life then was to show him my worth and prove it." Schwab was able to take the best of Jones and Carnegie, creating the new American industrialist. Schwab had a lovable personality that made him a very likable person. Schwab started a new era in industrial management.

This era was rooted in the success of the Industrial Victorians like Carnegie, but broke new ground. Charles Schwab can be considered an Industrial Edwardian, progressive on management but anchored to the past in union relations. In this view Schwab, the Industrial Edwardian, can be considered part of a natural evolution of the beliefs of the Industrial Victorians such as Carnegie, Morrell, Thomson, Fritz, Bessemer, Jones and Holley. Schwab would refine the managerial gifts of Jones, like Jones had refined the gifts of Morrell at Cambria. With Schwab, industrial chemistry was born. The birth of industrial chemistry would be another Braddock first. Schwab would also be the driving force behind the introduction of production planning and industrial engineering departments. Schwab would discover an array of new uses for steel. He would be the founder of the two largest steel companies of the era: United States Steel and Bethlehem Steel. Most important, like Jones, Schwab would develop a long line of "Braddock" managers who would not only transform the steel industry, but American industry.

Charles Schwab was the "eldest" of Bill Jones's boys of Braddock. Schwab would change the face of the American Steel industry using the basic concepts of Bill Jones. Schwab was the architect of the formation of United States Steel. He would be the first president of United States Steel Corporation. Later as president of Bethlehem Steel, he would build it into the number two steel maker. In the European press Schwab became the "Crown Prince of Steel." Schwab became a mover and shaker in American industry, being the catalyst in the formation of such companies as International Nickel. Biographer, Robert Hessen, said, "Perhaps the greatest symbols of Schwab's life can be seen from the center of Park Avenue in New York City, as one looks up at skyscrapers built with the Bethlehem beam." He never forgot the birthplace of his wife and his adopted home, Braddock. He made many gifts to Braddock, including St. Thomas Catholic Church. St. Thomas has a great deal of personal meaning for me. My grandfather was the first to be baptized there and my grandmother the last to be buried from St. Thomas. For years I traveled from Michigan to meet the whole Skrabec/Finnerty family at Midnight Mass. Many of the gifts of Carnegie and Schwab would affect generations of Braddock residents but may have been lost to the original audience.

Schwab would ultimately receive ten honorary doctorates. He won the French Legion of Honor as well as the Bessemer medal from the British Iron and Steel Institute. He pioneered the use of industrial chemistry and metallurgical science. However, his biggest contribution, like that of his mentor Jones, was the development of the great managerial pool of the "boys of Braddock." Schwab would package the spirit of Bill Jones as a model for young managers. Jones and Schwab together revolutionized how American managers function.

Schwab was very clear on success. In a speech to a trade school graduating class in 1901, Schwab spelled out his path for success: "success is not money alone"; "start early"; "exceed your duties"; "effort, not backing is the key to promotion"; and "go win on your own merits." Schwab was at his best talking to young men going into the trades.

Like his mentor Jones, Schwab was a community man and was very generous to the people of Braddock. He donated a number of fire trucks as well as churches of various denominations. Schwab totally financed an outstanding brass band. Community and good living conditions were part of the Schwab approach to managing. Also like Jones, Schwab loved to gamble but he was known to deliberately lose large bets with friends who had fallen on hard times. Clearly Schwab had the same enlarged heart of Jones. His Saturday night Braddock poker games became famous as well.

Charles Schwab came to Braddock in 1879 from the small Pennsylvania town of Loretto. Braddock at the time was a town of 9,000.[1] Schwab was wearing his first suit with a five-dollar note pinned on the inside by his mother. He had come to be a clerk in a grocery store near the entrance to Edgar Thomson Works, McDevitt's. The Braddock that Charles Schwab came to was then a town of opportunity and dreams. It was a town of bars and frustration as well. McDevitt's was the store where Bill Jones bought his cigars. Jones and Schwab hit it off right away. Jones loved Schwab's quick wit and sharp humor. About to lose his job at McDevitt's, it was Bill Jones that got him started at the steel works. That was September 12, 1879. It was typical of the Braddock tradition (and very Carnegian) that a young volunteer soldier would rise to be a great general.

Schwab was Jones trained but he had his own personality. He was a happy person. "Those who remember him say he was the happiest boy in the village-laughing, whistling, singing."[2] It was a personality trait that made him popular among employees, bosses, suppliers and customers. He gained the nickname "Smiling Charlie." Schwab was a master of positive motivation. In many parts of the mill there was a no-smoking safety policy. Schwab was always fond of touring the mill. In his unannounced tours he found many violators of the policy. While most managers would dismiss or punish the worker, Schwab would give the worker one of the fine cigars he carried, telling worker to save it for outside of work.

It was in Braddock that Schwab found and married Rana Dinkey. While Jones had started Schwab out in the engineering department, he quickly needed more money. One of his side jobs was to teach piano to the two children of Bill Jones. Schwab idealized three men in his life: Napoleon, Carnegie and Bill Jones.

---

[1] Robert Hessen, *Steel Titan–The Life of Charles M. Schwab* (New York: Oxford Press, 1975), 13
[2] Casson, 156

Emma Eurania (Rana) Dinkey was from one of the earliest Braddock families. The Dinkeys were seventeenth-century immigrants from Alsace-Lorraine. This small country would bring a number of immigrants to the Braddock area. Actually the Dinkeys didn't arrive at Braddock from eastern Pennsylvania until the opening of Edgar Thomson Works in 1875. Mrs. Dinkey, a widow, came to Braddock to open a boarding house. Charles Schwab ended up boarding there. Her son Alva Dinkey would become one of the "boys of Braddock." Alva was the boyhood friend of Charles Schwab and would have the helping hand of Schwab throughout his career. Alva started in Edgar Thomson's machine shop and by forty-seven was a millionaire and president of Carnegie Steel.

In many aspects Schwab would become a blend of his idols, Jones and Carnegie. Schwab had the drive of both and the social skills of Napoleon. There were differences. Schwab was reader and a lover of science. In the application of science, Schwab would differ from Jones. We have seen that Jones was not interested in hard sciences such as chemistry. Still market pressure for this technology was increasing. Carnegie's partner, Phipps, had already pioneered the application of chemistry in the running of Lucy Furnaces. Phipps had been the first to employ a chemist at an iron works. Phipps recalled: "What fools we had been! But then there was this consolation: we were not as great as fools as our competitors.... Years after we had taken chemistry to guide us said they could not afford to employ a chemist. Had they known the truth then, they would have known they could not afford to be with out one."[3] J. Edgar Thomson, president of the Pennsylvania Railroad, had early on in his career taken an interest in chemistry. By 1875, Thomson, then president of the Pennsylvania Railroad, was ordering rails to precise chemical specifications.

---

[3] Livesay, 114

A young Schwab, like Carnegie's partner Phipps, realized that steel chemistry would be the future of steel making. Schwab later recalled: "In my own house I rigged up a laboratory and studied chemistry in the evenings, determined that there should be nothing in the manufacture of steel that I would not know. Although I had received no technical education I made myself master of chemistry and of the laboratory, which proved of lasting value."[4] Schwab would do chemical analysis of steel at home and check his results against the Edgar Thomson lab results. Schwab's studies even went further. He tried to relate steel properties to steel chemistry. He even studied the corrosive effects of industrial acids on steel. This boyhood interest in chemistry was shared with one of Schwab's old friends in later life-Thomas Edison. When Henry Phipps heard of Schwab's experiments, he gave Schwab a thousand dollars to improve his home laboratory. The roots of the great USS Corporation research center in Monroeville, Pennsylvania, can be traced to this boyhood lab of Charles Schwab.

Schwab would even win over Jones to the need of chemistry in steel making. Later Schwab would ultimately be the first to start to hire professional chemists at Edgar Thomson Works. One of them was James Gayley, who would become the first vice president of United States Steel. Another of the "boys of Braddock" was Braddock-born William Corey, also a chemist, who became the second president of United States Steel. Two other friends and Braddock chemical lab employees, Alva Dinkey and David Kerr, would ultimately become vice-presidents of United States Steel as well. Chemistry would become a central part of Schwab's career, expanding steel applications and improving product and process. Schwab installed the first metallurgical and chemical laboratory in industry at Edgar Thomson Works. As with his

---

[4] Hessen, 27

own early chemistry experiments, Schwab would build the foundation for product research at United States Steel. By the end of his career, Schwab had opened the executive ranks to the industrial chemist making Works Chief Chemist a key position on the executive ladder.

Schwab had started at Edgar Thomson Works in the engineering department. He had taken some engineering courses, which he played up to Jones. He began as a survey crewmember. In a few years as chief engineer, he built the Bessemer tunnel connecting Edgar Thomson Works directly to Port Perry. This tunnel today remains in operation and is destined to become a historical landmark in Allegheny County. Schwab moved up rapidly under Captain Jones. After a year he was assistant plant manager. One of his key duties was to run messages to Carnegie in Pittsburgh. Schwab's personality again won Carnegie over and he moved to the partnership fast track. From 1880 to 1887, Charles Schwab was assistant works superintendent of Edgar Thomson under Bill Jones. Illinois Steel, Duquesne Steel and Pittsburgh Bessemer Steel at Homestead would challenge Edgar Thomson Works and the Carnegie empire during this period. Duquesne and Pittsburgh Steel companies were in sight of Edgar Thomson works. Carnegie's plan was to break both and ultimately both became part of Carnegie's empire.

We shall look at Duquesne Steel first even though it was built after Pittsburgh Steel at Homestead. Duquesne Steel was built in 1886 (Homestead in 1882) right across the river from Braddock, where General Braddock had first mustered his troops for the attack on Braddock's Field. Duquesne Steel failed quickly and was reorganized into Allegheny Bessemer Steel. Allegheny was formed by a group of anti-Carnegie iron barons. It pioneered a new rolling process that briefly allowed the Allegheny Bessemer to produce rails at lower costs than Edgar Thomson!

A direct rolling process achieved this brief competitive success. At Edgar Thomson ingots were first broken down on a blooming mill producing an intermediate bloom, which had to be reheated and rolled to a rail in the rail mill. At Allegheny a process was developed to roll direct from ingot to rails, skipping the intermediate bloom. Direct rolling substantially reduced costs. In addition the plant hired the lowly paid Hungarians and Slavs of the Edgar Thomson banned Amalgamated union. Carnegie could not allow such a challenge by the Pittsburgh iron aristocracy in his backyard. What evolved was a classic application of social Darwinism in business.

First Carnegie used a devious marketing campaign. Carnegie wrote the railroads warning them that direct rolling produced defective rails, which might lead to safety concerns. Secondly Carnegie worked with his railroad network to block the purchase of rails from Allegheny Bessemer. Providence also came to Carnegie's aid with an economic downturn. By 1890 Allegheny Bessemer was nearly bankrupt and was causing the partners to keep infusing new cash into the operation. Carnegie and his new partner Frick then moved to purchase Allegheny Bessemer. The purchase is considered a classic business takeover as historian Peter Krass reported, "The purchase became a coup of legend within the industry. Instead of paying cash, Carnegie issued five-year bonds; by the time the bonds came due in 1895, the plant had paid for itself six times over. Never before or after was there such a bargain, and Carnegie again triumphed over Pittsburgh's iron aristocracy."[5]

With Allegheny Bessemer, now called Duquesne Works, in hand, Charles Schwab was sent to study the direct rolling process. Schwab verified the product reliability and the cost savings. Schwab then re-designed Edgar Thomson Works to

---

[5] Krass, 265

direct roll. Edgar Thomson Works with direct rolling became the first integrated continuous process mill. It would now move direct from iron ore to a finished rail. The Homestead threat would prove more challenging to Carnegie.

The Homestead rail mill was about a mile downriver from Braddock and it would challenge both Carnegie and Braddock's supremacy in steel. Carnegie competitors had built it five years before Schwab became superintendent. Homestead originated from the old Pittsburgh iron aristocracy as well. It was a group that had been run over by Andrew Carnegie. Old partner Andrew Kloman headed up the Homestead group of Pittsburgh iron makers aimed at overtaking Carnegie before economies of scale would prevent competition in the iron and steel industry. On October 12, 1879, these iron barons formed the Pittsburgh Bessemer Steel Company to produce rails. This was to be a Bessemer plant on the scale of Edgar Thomson. William Clark, one of the few major plant designers not under Carnegie's control, was hired to build and run it. Clark was an old line Industrial Victorian, tough on labor. The Amalgamated Association of Iron and Steel Workers, having been beaten at Edgar Thomson Works, planned to take Homestead from day one. Clark's first error was with front line management. Clark, an Englishman, favored the Welsh as operating foremen over the Irish. The Irish had always controlled the hot metal end and this caused a great deal of anger. Clark furthermore tried to follow Edgar Thomson Works's success in requiring non-union contracts (yellow-dog contracts) from the workers. The yellow dog contract was outlawed in the 1930s (with the help of the boys of Braddock). The problem was that Clark was dealing with a lot of ex-Edgar Thomson employees, who would not back down. These outlawed union men were determined to unionize Homestead. This time the union, learning from Carnegie having gained the upper hand in a maintenance shutdown at Edgar Thomson Works, waited to move when the Homestead plant was in full operation. The owners quickly backed down.

This initial volley by the union at Homestead was only the start of years of labor struggle. The Kloman management group countered a few months later with dismissal of Amalgamated workers. This resulted in a series of small strikes at the Homestead plant. The Amalgamated Union had 70,000 workers nationwide, controlling all of the iron industry and most of the steel industry.[6] The Amalgamated Association of Iron, Steel and Tin Workers was formed in August 1876 by a merger of three iron and steel unions. These three were: the United Sons of Vulcan (mainly puddlers), the Associated Brotherhood of iron and Steel Heaters, Rollers and Roughers, and the Steel Roll Hands of the United States. These three unions represented the highest paid mill workers, in particular the puddlers and rollers. A major exception was the Edgar Thomson Works, which had blocked any real control by the Amalgamated. To work at Edgar Thomson Works a worker had to sign an agreement not to be a member of the Amalgamated Union. The Amalgamated certainly had the power to strike Pittsburgh iron industries, which were Carnegie competitors. Amalgamated power was reinforced when it joined other unions at a Pittsburgh convention in 1881. This union alliance was called the Federation of Organized Trade and Labor Unions. The organization would become the American Federation of Labor (AFL). The Pittsburgh convention linked the Knights of Labor with the Amalgamated in 1882, which was to be the root of today's United States Steelworkers. The combination gave the Amalgamated union the national and regional strength needed to take the major part of the steel industry, but little of Carnegie's empire.

---

[6] Bridge, 154

The back and forth at Homestead Works continued with no progress on either side until the union called for a strike. On June 1, 1882, the Amalgamated and the new worker alliance called for the first national steel strike. The Amalgamated successfully paralyzed the industry across the nation, with the exception of Braddock's Edgar Thomson Works. Carnegie was pretty much on the sidelines during this national strike. Carnegie was able to watch and wait as the new Homestead company and his competitors struggled with the union. The long series of shutdowns and strikes weakened the Pittsburgh Bessemer Steel Company at Homestead, which had lost early on its spiritual leader with the death of Kloman in 1880. The remaining iron barons crushed by stoppages, strikes and financial losses could no longer maintain the Homestead plant. In October 1883 with no place to go, they sold out to Carnegie. The union had played into the Carnegie strategy to take over Homestead's Pittsburgh Bessemer Steel Company.

Actually the great "Homestead" works was to be built beside the Edgar Thomson Works. Carnegie had made the decision to add the structural mill in Braddock in 1886 before the Homestead mill went on the market. Carnegie and Schwab had already started experiments at Edgar Thomson using an open hearth. Carnegie recalled in his *Autobiography*, "We had about concluded in 1886 to build alongside of the Edgar Thomson Mills, new works for the manufacture of miscellaneous shapes of steel when it was suggested to us that the five or six leading manufacturers of Pittsburgh, who had combined to build the works at Homestead, were willing to sell their mills to us."

Homestead was built as a Bessemer rail mill to compete with Edgar Thomson Works. Carnegie did not need any more rail capacity when he purchased Homestead. His immediate goal with the purchase of Homestead was to drive out the competition for Edgar Thomson Works. In 1886, he decided to re-design Homestead to be a structural mill for the construction industry. Homestead would make structural shapes such as building beams and armor plate. The market demand for structural steel was growing but the demand for higher quality was also growing. The Bessemer process's main limitations were its inability to remove phosphorus and sulfur. These two impurities in steel can greatly reduce mechanical properties such as strength and the ability to resist impact. A new steel making process was now available in the open-hearth furnace or the Siemens process. Carnegie decided to fully convert and rebuild Homestead Works to be an open-hearth shop.

Again we must continue our metallurgy course to understand the open-hearth process at Homestead. When we discussed sulfur, phosphorus and the Bessemer process, we talked of controlling sulfur and phosphorus impurities in the ores, and coke as a means of controlling final Bessemer steel content. The market demand for quality was calling for even lower impurity content. The Germans, in particular, were blocked out of using the Bessemer process because of their high phosphorus ores. Economic need in Germany led to the development of a new process by Charles Siemens. The open-hearth furnace was like a huge puddling furnace. It was a shallow brick hearth. The hearth was heated by hot gas. Like the Bessemer process, the open hearth used liquid pig iron from the blast furnaces. The bath of liquid pig iron is then "worked" by slag of limestone. It is a chemical process requiring chemical control and sampling: a process Charles Schwab was prepared to manage because of his chemical expertise. The hot slag flows on the top of the liquid iron and removes sulfur and phosphorus. Englishman, Sidney Gilchrist-Thomas, covered the chemical process under a patent.

Carnegie actually had obtained the patent for the Thomas process back in 1881. Carnegie had foreseen the demand for higher quality and the limitations of the Bessemer process. He had experimented at Edgar Thomson with the Bessemers using the Thomas process 1886. Schwab was involved in these trials because of his chemical knowledge. The experiments were never successful; the egg-shaped Bessemer vessel did not allow for enough surface to work the slag and activate the chemical reactions. A small experimental open-hearth furnace was built at Edgar Thomson Works to develop the future process of Homestead. Julian Kennedy, Braddock's furnace wizard, was involved in these early experiments. These experiments at Braddock of Julian Kennedy would form the basis of a re-design of Homestead Works.

The open-hearth process had many other advantages. First the top size of a Bessemer furnace was 15 tons while the open-hearth furnace could process fifty tons. The open hearth could use lower grade ores such as those in the huge Mesabi Range in Michigan. The chemical nature of the process was its real strength. It allowed for analysis and steel alloying as well as removal of impurities. Phipps and Schwab, both amateur chemists, were the biggest supporters. Carnegie in fact sent Schwab to visit the great open-hearth plants of Europe.

The best open-hearth mills in the world were at Krupp Iron Works in Essen, Germany. Essen was the only other city in the world that could claim the title of steel city from Braddock. Krupp had solved some difficult chemical problems. First Krupp had been successful in making the Thomas process work in a Bessemer converter. The German success was related to the use of limestone and dolomite refractory bricks. In addition like Carnegie, Krupp purchased low phosphorus and sulfur ore supplies. Still Krupp quickly embraced the new open-hearth process, applying what they learned about the power of limestone and dolomite to remove impurities. Schwab was able to pick up some key operating practices on his visit to Krupp Works. Carnegie as usual wanted to apply the best technology and the biggest equipment available in the re-building of Homestead. Furthermore Carnegie brought in the best men such as Edgar Thomson's furnace wizard, Julian Kennedy. Under the guidance of Kennedy, the first American open-hearth shop was erected at Homestead in 1886. The shop consisted of two fifty-ton basic furnaces. Such a shop overshadowed any Bessemer shop, which at the time had a maximum capacity of 15 tons per furnace. These two giant open hearths at Homestead, when tapped together were famous for producing 100-ton forgings for Homestead's twelve-ton press. Homestead would become the biggest structural and plate mill in the world. Homestead would armor a new American Navy with steel ships. The plates for the famous battleship, *Maine,* were made at Homestead in 1889.While Homestead became the Jerusalem of open-hearth steel making, it was a flawed plant in Carnegie's mind.

The problem at Homestead, however, was not technology. The Amalgamated Association of Iron, Steel, and Tin Workers had dug in at Homestead. Carnegie realized he would need a manager who had popularity with the workers. Based on Jones's recommendation, Carnegie named Schwab General Superintendent of Homestead in 1886, moving him from Assistant Superintendent for Bill Jones at Edgar Thomson Works. Schwab's assistant would be John Potter, one of the Edgar Thomson boys, who had worked his way up from a "Greaser Boy" (a person who oils and lubricates machinery). It was Schwab's outstanding ability to work with people that initially kept Homestead from exploding. In fact Schwab was breaking tonnage and rolling records from the start at Homestead.

The first confrontation, under Carnegie's ownership, with the powerful Amalgamated was in the spring of 1889 at Homestead. Carnegie was interested in applying a sliding wage scale. The sliding wage scale was based on the price that

Carnegie could get for his steel rails. If the price went down the workers would be paid less for the same amount of work. The struggle resulted in a strike. Eventually a compromise was reached that allowed a modified sliding scale for the acceptance of the union. The Amalgamated Association of Iron, Steel and Tin Workers set up the model for today's union shops. There was a "committee man" in each department to represent the union. Hiring and firing required the approval of the union. At Braddock, Jones held the union out of Edgar Thomson Works. The unofficial system of nationalities "lodges" at Edgar Thomson Works was the system copied by the Amalgamated. Both Edgar Thomson's lodge system and the Amalgamated Union at Homestead favored the Irish (furnace jobs), Welsh and Germans (rolling) as well as small groups of English and Scottish. The low-wage labor jobs of the Slavs and Hungarians (plus a few blacks) were not represented. This first Homestead strike was, however, a great union victory in the long run. Carnegie and his new partner, Henry Clay Frick, would take on the union again in three years.

With the death of Bill Jones on September 28, 1889, in a fiery furnace accident, Braddock needed a new leader. Charles Schwab moved back to his beloved "ET." Carnegie did not want to move his now best-loved manager back to Braddock but with Schwab's persistence, he relented. Had Schwab stayed in Homestead, the face of the industry might have been different. Homestead historian William Searin put it this way, "Schwab's move to Edgar Thomson as Jones's successor was perhaps unfortunate for the Carnegie enterprises, for Schwab had been a big hit with the Homestead men. Had he stayed at Homestead he might have found a way to avert the labor-management confrontation that was soon to erupt there."[7]

---

[7] William Serrin, *Homestead* (New York: Times Books, 1992), 53

Charles Schwab, as general superintendent of Edgar Thomson Works, continued the focus on production. The number of employees grew to 3500 in 1890. Schwab added two blast furnaces. The plant averaged 54,782 tons of pig iron monthly from the battery of blast furnaces. Edgar Thomson Works continued to be the biggest steel plant in the world. He added a second rail rolling mill. Edgar Thomson blast furnaces continued to break tonnage records.

Schwab was different from Jones in that he liked living high. At Homestead, Schwab was forced to live in a row of manager houses near the mill. These houses were stark and in the dirt of the mill. Schwab's biographer, Robert Hessen, described it as: "The house was small, it had no bathroom, and its only sources of heat were coal grates and the kitchen stove." Edgar Thomson Works had a similar row of "executive" houses inside the mill, but they were not to be the house Schwab lived in. Schwab would build the "superintendent's mansion" in North Braddock. He hired famous Pittsburgh architect, Fredrick Osterling, to build the house as well as his gift to the community, St. Thomas Catholic Church. Osterling was one of the first designers of the great steel skyscrapers. He also built the Cape May Hotel in New Jersey. The Braddock mansion was a beautiful house that still stands today. In addition Osterling built St. Francis in Loretto, Pennsylvania, as a donation to Schwab's hometown. Schwab liked the good life and that would cause many problems for him.

However, Schwab was soon to show that he was up to his mentor's old job. The major cost problem at Edgar Thomson Works was the production of "distressed" steel, as well as "seconds," which was substandard steel. This was steel that did not meet quality standards to be shipped on orders. These "seconds" would eventually sell at a lower price, reworked at additional cost to be made prime material or scrapped. Like

Jones, Schwab believed in the power of competition. Schwab felt that arousing the inherent competitiveness of the men could solve problems like substandard steel. In the case of substandard steel, Schwab focused on crew competitiveness between shifts. Schwab offered a cash bonus of twenty dollars to the workers of the crew with the lowest amount of substandard steel. The results were, as Schwab suspected, a dramatic reduction in substandard steel.

Another problem for Schwab was the new Carnegie partner, Henry Clay Frick. Frick became president of Carnegie's steel interests. Frick was already a millionaire owner of a major coke supplier to Carnegie's operations. Frick was tough on labor. He was cold and uncaring but was a legendary cost cutter, which attracted Carnegie to him. Carnegie's biographer, Harold Livesay, wrote, "Frick never seemed to regret anything he did. He had that most dangerous of all human qualities, a belief in the rightness of his own actions. All of his actions. At all times." Frick was not interested in motivating workers but only in keeping costs down. Frick was the classic Industrial Victorian, interested and believing in technology with little interest in the human element. Frick hated unions to the point of being obsessed with crushing them. He saw nothing in the good treatment of the workingman.

Like Jones, Schwab believed that it wasn't the money but the competition that motivated the workers. Many times Jones had pointed out to Schwab that some form of recognition was required. A simple verbal congratulation might work as well as money. Schwab, however, was a stronger administrator and wanted more formalized programs. Schwab was above all a people person; he believed in the human spirit.

More challenging for Schwab as the superintendent of Edgar Thomson was the growing labor strife across the river at Homestead. Homestead was a hotbed of unionism and

Edgar Thomson had held out the union. However, Edgar Thomson Works was the only works to have the sliding scale in place. In 1890, the rail market was highly depressed, driving down wages that were tied to rail prices. Homestead, while unionized, did not fall under the sliding scale under the terms gained in the earlier strike settlement. Edgar Thomson's wage fell to below living wages. As a result the Amalgamated union was starting to gain support at Edgar Thomson. The Amalgamated union had coupled with the remnants of the secret Knights of Labor still in the Braddock community.

Schwab hated the sliding wage scale but he was also, like Jones, fundamentally opposed to unions. Unions seemed in opposition to his theory of motivation. Schwab summarized his views: "Under the labor-union system all members are reduced to a dead level of equality, and the wage scale largely is determined by the worth and capability of the cheapest workman, instead of the most capable and highest priced. This narrows opportunity, dulls ambition and gives no man a chance to rise."[8] Jones and Schwab were not anti-worker but anti-union. The press and historians often fail to understand the difference. Schwab believed and promoted the dream of no limit to people with ambition and drive. Like Jones, Schwab believed that dream should be open to even the lowest laborer. Frick was more representative of the other extreme view of the Industrial Victorians. Frick was cold to the problems of the men; they were but inputs into the manufacturing process.

Schwab was torn between supporting the men, appeasing the demands of new President Frick and a distrust of unions. At the end of 1890, the tensions at Braddock reached a crisis point. The record-breaking blast furnace department had a 30 percent increase in output. The sliding scale because of the low market price required a wage decrease for the very men that had set new production records. A delegation from the

---

[8] Hessen, 131

furnaces met with Schwab asking for an end to the sliding scale and a wage increase. The request made sense to Schwab's managerial approach. Schwab, however, was less forceful with superiors than Jones. Clearly, Schwab's desire to please his superiors had a downside. Schwab was the great compromiser and he tried to convince Frick to increase the wages. Failing to convince Frick, Schwab fell in line. Schwab had trouble dealing with Frick because he was not one of Carnegie's original six or one of the "boys." The end result was a strengthening of the Amalgamated and rising support for a strike.

This move at Edgar Thomson was another of many Frick managerial mistakes. Edgar Thomson was the Carnegie flagship and it had always held the Carnegie line. The men reluctantly had supported Carnegie on the twelve-day and sliding scale. Edgar Thomson had stayed out of national union strikes, which had bankrupted Carnegie's competition. Edgar Thomson was still the most productive plant in the world. The men were truly hurting. Carnegie was still reporting a profit. Only a resentful and less than capable manager would take such a hardheaded stand on a minor wage increase as Frick.

Frick would show that his style was to resist demands and union threats. Frick had been hardened by the strikes of the Amalgamated in his Pennsylvania coal operations. Great granddaughter Martha Frick Symington Singer described Frick's union battles at his coke works: "The Hungarians and Slavs who worked in those coke works refused to work at the price that the H. C. Frick Coke Company was paying. They not only refused to work for it they refused to allow anybody else to work. And so, as my great-grandfather began to bring people in to work, they marched on the Morewood plant, not once, but twice and ah, in the middle of the night, and ah, to sound of beating drums, they were absolutely drunk, they were armed with guns, and pipes, and shovels, and brooms. They burned up all the coking tools, they tore the fence down and they did you know hundreds of thousands if not millions of dollars worth of damage. And for my great-grandfather this was intolerable. And he did say, these are ignorant people, they are not naturalized American citizens, they do not speak English. They are ignorant tools of the labor leaders, he said always; well, what is going to rule our great commonwealth? The law or mob violence?" Frick's coalmine experience had clearly hardened him to any requests of the union at Edgar Thomson Works.

Schwab calculated that to give the blast furnace department at Edgar Thomson Works the wages they had asked for would cost the company $28,344 per year. Considering that Carnegie Steel profits for 1890 were over $4.8 million, from a mere financial standpoint it was the right thing to do.[9] On a broader scale it should have been a "no brainer." Edgar Thomson was the corporate flagship and was non-union. Furthermore, Edgar Thomson was the productivity leader for the company. To short-change the flag bearer would give the union new motivation. Still Frick decided to hold his ground.

The deadline at Edgar Thomson Works was set for New Year's Day, 1891. Schwab braced for a fight. Schwab wanted to call in the Pinkerton guards. Schwab knew the men, and some form of confrontation was unavoidable. Schwab considered asking Braddock saloonkeepers to close, but that would be too much to ask on a New Year's Eve night. It also would have been a huge task since every other building in Braddock was a bar. Besides, drinking inside the mill on holidays was commonplace. It would have been impossible to prevent drinking on New Year's Eve. Booze, however, as in the days of the Whiskey Rebellion muster at Braddock, would raise tensions. At midnight a group of stockyard Hungarians attacked the stockyards and caused a great deal of damage.

---

[9] Krass, 271

The Hungarians tended to be the lower paid workers who suffered most from the sliding wage scale. The Irish had the high skilled jobs in the furnaces while the Hungarians had the low paying unskilled and dangerous jobs. The Hungarians were also supportive of the Amalgamated union which had organized the Hungarians in the Pennsylvania coalfields.

Schwab raised a force of loyal men, mainly Irish, to break up the attack and protect the heart of the works, the blast furnaces. Most of these were Irish skilled furnace men. The Irish furnace lodge at Edgar Thomson had always been the heart of Jones's earlier support against unionization. By early morning the word of the midnight attack was spreading throughout the local Hungarian bars. By noon on New Year's Day, a new mob of 250 Hungarians moved to attack the blast furnaces. James Gayley, one of the "Braddock boys" and future vice-president of USS, was the blast furnace superintendent. Gayley and Schwab put together an armed group of loyal workers. Schwab and Gayley's loyalists held back the attack but a number of Hungarians were wounded and later would die. Again the site of this first labor death in the Monongahela valley would be on the very center of Braddock's Defeat where the blast furnaces had been built.

It was a terrible experience for both Schwab and Gayley, who were the two proudest followers of Bill Jones. Gayley had been with Bill Jones at Crane Works and eventually came to Edgar Thomson Works by the request of Bill Jones. He had followed the great furnace wizard and "Braddock" boy, Julian Kennedy, as blast furnace superintendent at Edgar Thomson in 1885. Gayley had rewritten the Edgar Thomson blast furnace records in the years from 1885 to 1889. Now he and Schwab had been involved in a fight with very men who were part of setting those records.

The 1889 New Year's Eve uprising at Braddock was quickly quieted. Schwab called it "not anything more than a drunken Hungarian spree." Frick and Carnegie downplayed it in New York. The company town, Braddock, kept it among family and the local press glossed it over. Yet it was a prelude to the Homestead Strike of 1892. It strengthened Frick in his ways. The magic of Schwab and Gayley is that by the end of the year, Edgar Thomson blast furnaces were again setting new records.

Across the river at Homestead, labor unrest continued as a daily problem. The union had watched closely the New Year's Eve uprising at Edgar Thomson Works. It was clear that Frick was out to break the union throughout the Carnegie mills. The Homestead contract was due to expire on July 1, 1892. Amazingly Carnegie and Frick had learned nothing from the Braddock New Year's Day Uprising. Frick intended to further reduce the pay out of the hated sliding scale. Frick also read the situation at Homestead wrong. Homestead was not Braddock where the spirit of Bill Jones and Schwab's managerial skills caused more plant loyalty than union loyalty. Homestead was the flagship of the union. The superintendent of Homestead, John Potter, was a Frick man. Carnegie was in Scotland at the time. With Carnegie out, the strike progressed from a disagreement to a national news event.

On June 24, 1892, after the union turned down a 15 percent wage reduction, Frick closed the plant seven days before the deadline. It was announced that the plant would open again on July 6. This was the start of the famous and bloody Homestead Strike of 1892. The tactic was partially successful in that only 325 of 3800 workers remained on strike on the plant reopening. This was a victory in itself, since the union had 1800 members at Homestead. Frick reinforced the plant with 300 Pinkerton guards. The strikers, seeing the Pinkertons coming down the Monongahela from their Braddock encampment, prepared to prevent their landing. The arrival of the Pinkertons bought solidarity to the union members. A shot was fired and a bloody battle followed which made national headlines. A total of thirteen men died and more than a hundred were wounded.

One of the deaths was from the "Braddock Artillery." Large crowds of steel workers from Rankin's Carrie Furnaces and Edgar Thomson Works were watching the struggle across river. Pinkertons were being brought by boat from Braddock and the wounded were being treated at Braddock Hospital. Some of these workers took a Civil War cannon from the G.A.R. Hall in Braddock and started to fire it at the Pinkerton boats with makeshift balls. The Homestead strikers cheered the Braddock artillery on until one of the balls sheared the head off a striker. The bloodbath was an embarrassment to Carnegie and a mark on Frick that he carried for life. The Homestead strike showed where Frick stood. Frick's view was simply, "We had to teach our employees a lesson and we have taught them one they will never forget." Carnegie secretly blamed Frick and Homestead superintendent, John Potter.

Carnegie's answer to this national scandal was to move Schwab to Homestead. In a letter to a partner Carnegie detailed his strategy: "Potter should be sent aboard and Schwab back to Homestead. He manages men well and would soon draw around him good men from E.T. [Edgar Thomson] and other works. Have suggested this to Frick."[10] Carnegie later in his autobiography noted: "Had he [Charles Schwab] remained at Homestead works, in all probability no serious trouble would have arisen. "Charlie" liked his work men and they liked him; but still remained at Homestead an unsatisfactory element in the men who had previously been discarded from other works for good reasons and had found employment at the new works before we purchased them." Carnegie was probably in error believing Schwab could have

---

[10] Hessen, 39

avoided a strike. In fact it might have been impossible for even Bill Jones. The problem was clearly at Frick's level.

In October, Schwab was moved back to Homestead. Schwab wanted badly to stay at Braddock. To persuade Schwab to move back, Frick offered him his first ownership in Carnegie Steel. Carnegie wanted this bad press behind him and he was counting on Schwab. Schwab's own statement on going back to Homestead was less optimistic: "During the great strike of 1892 I was asked, much against my wishes, to reorganize and take charge of the Homestead Works. I finally consented to do so.... When I went to Homestead I found it in a thoroughly disorganized condition. The works were badly run down, and the men were unsuited to their work, and they did not have competent foremen. Now, the first four months of time at Homestead were devoted entirely to reorganization."[11] Still Schwab was the right man and up to the task. When the union formally ended the strike, Charles Schwab greeted each returning man individually. He started a series of small group and union leader meetings. He worked personally with everything he could quickly fix. Some suggested that he had talked 24 hours at a time. He kept his door open to hear any grievance. He walked around the mill constantly, stopping to talk to any worker who was interested. These walkthroughs were on all shifts. He moved into the small executive home inside the plant and is said to have never set foot outside the plant for four months. It was the type of response that Carnegie had hoped for and anything less would have fallen short.

Schwab instituted his famous Saturday morning superintendents meeting. These Homestead meetings were the formation of "boys of Braddock" that would later form the core of the formal organization, the Carnegie Veterans Association. Schwab would also expand it for all of Carnegie

---

[11] Hessen, 39

steel when he became president. It included Joseph Schwab, Schwab's brother and rolling superintendent, who had worked his way up at Edgar Thomson from draftsmen. Alva Dinkey, Electrical Superintendent and Braddock resident, boyhood friend of Schwab was also a member of the group. Alva had worked himself up from "water boy" at Edgar Thomson Works. William Corey, Armor superintendent and Braddock-born boyhood friend was another present at these lunches. This grew into a major affair each week, with outstanding luncheon menus. Still it was the type of personal management that worked for Schwab. In addition during the week, Schwab would visit unannounced various departments to follow up on reports.

While Schwab worked to rebuild morale at Homestead, John Potter was "exiled." Potter had started with Schwab at Edgar Thomson. Potter remained with Carnegie but was put in dead-end jobs. The boys, for his over-enthusiastic support of Frick, also isolated him. When Carnegie put Frick out of the group, Frick took Potter into his employ. He moved to South America as a mining consultant for Frick and Mellon in 1902. Potter returned to Los Angeles in 1914. In an effort to bring Potter back in communion with the boys, Potter was invited to the twenty-first meeting of the Carnegie Veterans Association in 1925. On December 18, the day of the meeting, Potter went to Carnegie Street in Los Angeles and shot himself in the head. Carnegie also blacklisted Frick and they broke the partnership in 1898. They spent their final years hating each other. In 1912 Carnegie tried to patch up the old wounds but Frick refused saying he would "see Carnegie in Hell which is where we both are going." Homestead remained a black mark on the Carnegie organization but it was a stepping stone for Charles Schwab.

Amazingly Schwab was winning back the men even with the king of the Industrial Victorians, Henry Frick, in overall command of Homestead in 1892. Workers' wages were actually reduced in the first year after the strike. Schwab, however, assured the men that he could end the sliding scale. Schwab continued to work behind the scenes with Frick and Carnegie on the elimination of the hated sliding wage scale. In 1894, the sliding scale was abolished. The twelve-hour shift continued, however. The twelve-hour shift never had the full backing of the union unless wages in moving to an eight-hour schedule could be maintained. The company was hardly ready to increase its expense by paying the same amount for four hours' less work. Eighteen hundred men who had applied for reinstatement were never rehired. Schwab had argued to rehire but in the end he followed the orders of Frick and Carnegie. The community was in disarray. Homestead historian, William Serrin, described conditions a few months after the strike had ended (December 1892): "many Homestead families were destitute. To help the children, Kaufmann Brothers, a Pittsburgh department store, sent each one a book and a box of candy for the holidays. The workers of McKeesport sent Homestead workers a thousand turkeys. Just before Christmas, Homestead schoolchildren were asked to write letters to Santa Claus saying what they wanted for Christmas. Almost all of them asked for shoes and other practical items."

Still Schwab, like Jones, hated the union and this limited him at times in building worker trust. Schwab agreed with Frick to hire company spies. These spies worked at Homestead and reported union activity to Schwab. The men were constantly on the watch to identify these company spies. One account by Homestead historian, William Serrin, is particularly interesting: "For a time, the Carnegie Steel Company sent spies a turkey each Christmas, but this practice was abolished when the Homestead workers realized that the company's agents could be identified by observing who received turkeys, which arrived by the express, the week before the holiday."[12]

Labor problems continued at Homestead even with Schwab's heroic efforts. Schwab never could win over the lower paid Hungarian and Slav workers. Part of this was his well-known New Year Eve (1889) clash with the Hungarians at the Edgar Thomson blast furnaces. Another issue was that the Hungarians had deep roots with the old Amalgamated union. The Amalgamated had been in a series of bitter strikes with Frick's coal companies. The Amalgamated continued its effort to unionize at Homestead and the managers continued to identify union sympathizers and fire them. William Corey, Schwab's boyhood friend in Braddock, acted as Schwab's axe man at Homestead. Corey was active in keeping any form of union out.

Schwab's vision for the plant was a world-class producer of steel products. In his talks with the workers, he shared the vision and that it would mean more jobs and higher pay in the long run. Frick was a stone wall but Carnegie always tended to reward and pay on performance. Part of that vision was to develop a new steel market in armor plate. Schwab had studied armor production at Krupp Works in Germany. The American government was encouraging steel makers to build armor plants by offering large contacts. Carnegie needed little encouragement ordering an armor mill to be built in Homestead Works. The armor department was to be headed by Schwab's boyhood Braddock friend, William Ellis Corey. The Coreys were Braddock's royal family of coal and steel.

The most challenging part of Schwab's service was not the rebuilding the Homestead plant but the "Great Armor Scandal." The scandal in itself is capable of filling a book. The short version is that armor flowed out of the Homestead plant at high profit. The Navy and ultimately the national press

---

[12] Serrin, 104

charged Homestead with the manufacture of inferior product, which was shipped. The mess soon became the headlines of the national press and a Congressional investigation was launched. Homestead Works and Carnegie Steel were found guilty and Schwab and Corey were suggested as having been behind it. President Cleveland and Carnegie negotiated behind the scenes. In the end the scandal was never really resolved. President Cleveland offered publicly to reduce the fine but announced: "I'll take no more plates from Schwab or Corey." Carnegie replied to Cleveland with the following famous statement: "Even the President of the United States can't tell me how to run my business." Loyalty was the code of the "boys of Braddock" and not even the President could cause a break in this.

Carnegie's defense of these two "boys of Braddock" was more than appropriate, it was the right thing to do. Schwab had always been a loyal lieutenant of the company. He followed Carnegie's orders regardless of his own beliefs. The testimony of Schwab was clear that he knew nothing of the discrepancies that must to some decree have occurred. The press as we see today had trouble believing that the top executive could be ignorant of wrongdoing. It does, however, point out a weakness in one of the fundamental motivational techniques of the "boys of Braddock." Setting goals and inspiring employees to meet these goals with money, promotions and other incentives was the core of their management style. They created a highly competitive environment. Wanting to please and achieve was praised as a virtue. It is interesting that Carnegie, Schwab and Bill Jones all admired Napoleon and studied his methods. You can see the roots of their approaches in that of Napoleon. Napoleon once said, "Half the people of the world are ambitious and seek their happiness in attaining honors.... The love of glory makes them desire positions of power, and take perilous risks, finding themselves enticed by this power of command."[13] Carnegie and the "boys of Braddock" stacked the deck, of course, by hiring only Napoleon driven people. The danger with humans in such a competitive environment is that some will always go overboard to achieve results. The armor scandal when looked at objectively had this type of dishonest over-achieving.

The scandal passed slowly but Schwab was still a favorite of Carnegie. In 1896, Carnegie offered Schwab the position of Vice-President of Carnegie Steel. Schwab turned it down. He wanted to manage men, not be a runner for the president. Within a year, John Leishman, then president of Carnegie Steel resigned and Schwab became president of America's largest company on April 17, 1897. It would bring him into the world of J. P. Morgan and New York capitalists.

Schwab would become the catalyst for a greater company, United States Steel (USS). Morgan was inspired by Schwab's speech on the future of the steel industry in New York in December of 1900. After a dinner speech in New York for a group of bankers, Morgan and Schwab met informally until 3:00 in the morning. In that meeting it is believed that USS was formed. Within a few weeks Schwab had convinced Carnegie to sell. The new company would be the first in America to have a capitalization of over a billion dollars. Ten companies were merged into this mega steel corporation. The largest was Carnegie Steel followed by Chicago's Federal Steel. On April 16, 1901, Charles Schwab at thirty-nine became president of United States Steel. The monster was described as: "U.S. Steel was not an operating company, but a holding company. It controlled 213 steel mills and transportation companies, including 78 blast furnaces; 41 iron ore mines and a fleet of 112 barges; as well as 57,000 acres of coal and coke properties in the Connellsville region of

---

[13] Alan Schom, *Napoleon Bonaparte* (New York: HarperCollins, 1997), 11

Pennsylvania, with nearly 1,000 miles of railroad tracks to service the region."[14]

The operating statistics were even more amazing five years after its formation. USS made three-fifths of all American Bessemer steel and open-hearth steel. It made more steel than the countries of England or Germany. The amount of steel made was a quarter of the world's production. USS made two-thirds of all American rails and wire rods, three-fifths of all steel beams. It had a fleet of one hundred ore ships. USS owned as much land as the states of Vermont, Massachusetts, and Rhode Island. The capitalization equaled one-thirteenth of all the world's manufacturers and one-tenth of all American manufacturers. This monster all started with Braddock's Edgar Thomson Works.

Schwab's problems, however, were just beginning. He was president of the company, but there was a chairman, Judge Elbert Gary. Gary was the Carnegie of Chicago, representing the western mills in the merger. He was a moneyman and a Morgan man. It was clear from the start that Schwab and Gary could not coexist. Gary was a lot like Carnegie; he was an Industrial Victorian. He opposed the unions but took an approach modeled after the Krupp Steel: company towns. Gary's approach, like Krupp's, was controlling. Gary's system became known as welfare capitalism. It, like the paternal systems prior, was not that of the workers, who felt they could best handle how their earnings were spent. Gary, not tarnished by the blood of Homestead, gets a more favorable view of his counter union movement (welfare capitalism) from labor historians.

At the formation of United States Steel, the Amalgamated Association of Iron, Steel, and Tin workers represented about half the members it had at the time of the Homestead strike.

---

[14] *Report of the Commissioner of Corporations on the Steel Industry* (1911), I, 131; Hessen, 123

Gary's program had further reduced membership in the early 1900s. Gary took on the union directly in July 1909 over the USS policy that all mills would be open shops. Open shops did not require the employee to join the union. In addition he threw in a pay cut for the steelworkers. The Amalgamated called a strike. It would be the longest steel strike in American history, going fourteen months. USS managed to run at 70% capacity, meeting customer orders. In the end the Amalgamated was crushed.

Labor leaders soon started to miss the "boys'" approach on labor. In the new company (USS), J. P. Morgan and Judge Gary were in control of the policy. During the crushing of the Amalgamated union, it was noted: "The labour leaders found that going to *Morgan was a different proposition from going to John Fritz or Captain "Bill" Jones.* 'Schwab treated us well—Morgan did not,' said one of the labor leaders as he came down the steps of Morgan's office. The probability is that Morgan knew the truth—knew that the Amalgamated Association was painted to look like iron, and treated the leaders accordingly. After an ineffective strike of two months or more, all the workmen returned to work."[15] Schwab had anti-union beliefs based on a philosophical point of individual motivation but he loved the men. Gary and Morgan used a false benevolence to control. This control via benevolence was different than the "boys'" paternal approach to labor. In the case of Gary and Morgan, it was a type of industrial slavery that reasoned that a loving master knew best for the workers. This was different than the approach of Jones and Schwab, who wanted to help, not own, the worker.

Schwab's biographer noted the importance of Schwab's Braddock days: "Schwab viewed his years at Carnegie Steel as the lost golden age, a period when he operated at full mental and physical efficiency, a time when those close to him

---

[15] Casson, 250

marveled at his limitless enthusiasm and endurance and repeatedly urged him not to overwork or over think."[16] With the formation of USS, Schwab's national impact was just beginning but these would be the most turbulent years of his life.

What was it about these golden days of Edgar Thomson Works that the "boys of Braddock" found strength and vision in? Edgar Thomson Works had in a few short years overtaken the world steel kingdoms of Britain and Germany. Such a rise in a nation's industrial strength is unprecedented in history. Even Japan's "industrial miracle" in the 1980s took twenty to thirty years. Historians in general have missed the industrial lessons offered that the "boys" felt were so sacred. Many say that Edgar Thomson Works had cheap immigrant labor but that advantage was small. Both England and Germany paid little more to their "skilled and experienced" labor. India, China and even Eastern Europe had cheap labor and the natural resources but failed to develop a competitive steel industry. What happened at Edgar Thomson Works was a miracle of spirit. Even with Carnegie's and Frick's misguided views on paying the workforce, the "boys" triumphed in productivity. Bill Jones believed in good wages as well did his student managers such as Schwab.

What was it then, did Schwab with his Edgar Thomson Works experience see beyond the earlier views of Jones? The following points might be called Schwab's concept of business for the Edgar Thomson Works.

1. Business Is Based On Networks
Schwab had learned while men are driven by competition, business is driven by cooperation. The Braddock plant itself was named after its future customer, Edgar Thomson. Carnegie's network of

---

[16] Hessen, 298

friends going back to boyhood was the basis of a huge customer-supplier cooperative network. Years later when Schwab was asked how he was able to obtain so many orders to supply steel to the New York building boom he said: "no trick at all, they were obtained through friendship." Even the internal workings of the employees revolved around a cooperative spirit while at times such people as Frick abused this.

2. Labor And Management Must Work Together To Assure Consistent Employment
Schwab and Jones were true visionaries in that steady employment at reasonable wages was a goal that both labor and management wanted. Carnegie failed to see how he could achieve this in times of recession. Labor had also failed to see that excessive wages actually put pressure on management to adjust during recession by cutting employment. Schwab saw correctly that business and personal employee goals had to be merged through corporate policy. It remains a continuing problem even today but the vision for a solution was offered by Bill Jones: "It should be the aim of the firm to keep the works running steadily. This is one of the secrets of Cambria's low wages. The workmen, taking year in and year out, do better at Cambria than elsewhere. On steady work you can calculate on low wages." A century later the Japanese used a form of life-long employment to assure steady work. A handful of new work companies today in America are applying such principles. The "boys" would themselves a century earlier try to test various ways of achieving the ideal of a united and cooperative organization.

3. Mutual Rewards Should Be Based On Profitability
Jones and Schwab had often fought with Carnegie and Frick on bonuses and employee rewards. The "boys of

Braddock" had learned from Carnegie the perpetual nature of productivity bonuses and corporate profitability. Carnegie had failed to fully implement his own success he had found in motivating his managers with stock and ownership. The "boys" would take a broader concept of Carnegie's basic principle to all employees. Schwab had developed and proved the theorem that individual productivity payments and profitability are linked. The price that has to be paid is large profits to the capitalists. Schwab like Carnegie believed profits to be the engine of not only success but also high employment.

4. The Role Of The Manager And Corporation Is Paternal
The corporation is to act as a father protecting and developing the employees. Living conditions, health and safety are fundamental functions that managers must care for. Many might disagree but it was a very successful approach. The "boys" would go on to give American industry it first safety and pension programs. They would also improve on the brutal working hours of the day. The paternal approach was always respectful of the worker. It was not condescending like the welfare approach of Gary's. The paternal approach allowed for help to be given without the type obligation suggested by a welfare approach.

5. Technology And Investment Should Be The First Application Of Profits
The Schwab approach was to continuously reduce product costs through the application of technology and process improvements. Edgar Thomson Works reduced product cost almost continuously over a fifty-year span. Money was poured back in. Carnegie had a very strict policy that 25% of profits went to dividends and the balance to plant improvement. Schwab would later show

at Bethlehem Steel that even when profits were lacking, borrowing should be used to reduce product costs through technology. I believe that if the American steel industry had adhered to a policy of re-investment in the plants during the fifties and sixties, the Japanese would never have been successful in the American market in the seventies and eighties.

6. Production And Productivity Bonuses Should Be Used In Place Of Base Wage Increase

This was a novel plan of Schwab, which adjusted to the economy in a more acceptable manner than Carnegie's sliding wage scale. Schwab was a promoter of rewarding the men in good times while protecting the company in bad economic times. Carnegie saw his sliding scale as "profit-sharing" but the possibility of a wage reduction was unacceptable to the workingman and union. Schwab's approach was a compromise.

Chapter 8

"So distribution should undo excess, and each man have enough."
  —*Carnegie's favorite quote from Shakespeare*

The Steel Town of Braddock

The town of Braddock started as a trading post and became a deserted battlefield. The earliest settlers were Irish and Scots-Irish. Some English purchased land after the Revolutionary War but generally the Irish farmed the land. The English, however, did bring the first blacks to Braddock as slaves. With the "whiskey tax" in the 1790s, a large number of Scots-Irish left the area for the new frontiers in Kentucky. The area was basically Irish farmers, a few German farmers, English landowners and a few black slaves. There were Indians in the area until 1820. The beginning of some mining of coal in the 1830s brought in some Welsh, Cornish, Austrians and some Germans from the Alsace-Lorraine area in Europe. The 1840s saw the numbers of Irish, Scots and English continue to increase. A few Dutch families came in from central Pennsylvania. In the late 1850s there was an influx of Germans. This second wave of German immigration was the Catholic Germans and Austrians escaping Catholic bigotry in Germany, in contrast to the first wave of Protestant German farmers. The Welsh, Cornish and Austrians were particularly adept at specialized mining techniques like the use of mine dogs. This later group of Austrians, Welsh and Germans were skilled workers fleeing political and economic struggles in Europe. The new settlers formed beachheads in the area to which more of their family and friends in Europe could immigrate. Austrians in particular were adept at forming colonies for immigrants.

Also in the late 1830s and 1840s some second and third generation native born Americans, mainly New Englanders, moved to the Braddock area to work on the lock and dam system for the Monongahela River. An example of this was the local patriarchal Corey family, who traced their roots back to the *Mayflower*. The Coreys actually came to Braddock via New London, Connecticut; Burlington, Vermont; and Jefferson City, Pennsylvania in a trip that took 170 years. They came to help build dam No. 2 on the Monongahela at Port Perry. Out of this family two Carnegie Steel executives would rise, with William Corey becoming the second president of United States Steel and founder of Midvale Steel and Ordnance (the company included Remington Arms). In addition, another branch of this family would start coal mining in Braddock with the Mellon family.

The first churches in Braddock reflect the nationalities. The earliest church was the Methodist Episcopal in then Port Perry started by the Corey family in 1848. St. Thomas Catholic Church was organized in 1854, as a missionary parish of Pittsburgh's St. Paul's to service the Irish in Braddock. As the mining, transportation industry and merchants increased so did the English, Scots and Welsh. These groups helped form the First United Presbyterian Church of Braddock in 1864.

Prior to the Civil War, the physical layout of the town started to change. This change occurred with the coming of the railroads. In 1859, the Pittsburgh and Connellsville Railroad was extended from the borough line at Port Perry through the town of Braddock. This took away the business area, which was on Halket Street. Ninth Street became the center for the merchants. Eventually the main street became Braddock Avenue, which was the old military road from Braddock to Fort Pitt.

During the Civil War, Braddock's Field became Fort Copeland. Since the Revolutionary War, it had been a military training area because of its location on old Braddock's Road and because of its river port. The tradition continued right into the 1890s when Pinkerton guards used the area as a camp. Fort Copeland trained soldiers for the war. At times the camp reached a population of 6,000.

The building of Edgar Thomson Works was the real beginning of Braddock as a town. The population of Braddock increased from 1,290 in 1870 to 19,357 in 1910. Braddock prior to Edgar Thomson Works was a rural farming community with some coal mining. There were only a few farmers' markets and one dry goods store.

With the start of Edgar Thomson Works, labor was extremely short and the first wave of immigrants came from England, Ireland and Germany. The biggest wave, however, came with Captain Bill Jones from the Johnstown area. Jones would bring in the first wave of Slavs and Hungarians as well as the first Poles, Russians and Italians. With the Pennsylvania Railroad in place and the mill starting up, one source of immigration was the railroad tramps that flowed in and stayed if work could be found. Since Braddock had a sparse population at the opening of the Edgar Thomson Works, there was not much tension between the nationalities in these early days. Some gangs had formed as early as the 1850s with the British native sons attacking the newly arrived Irish immigrants. Interestingly by the 1880s it would be the Irish gangs attacking the newly arrived Hungarians.

Braddock offered the "Romance of Millions" to young native Pennsylvanians like Charles Schwab. Schwab's biographer, Robert Hesson, described Schwab's arrival in 1879: "When Charles Schwab reached Braddock he was thrust into an unfamiliar and unwholesome environment. Loretto [Schwab's Pennsylvania home town] was a sleepy hamlet of whose 300 inhabitants shared a common life-style and religion; Braddock was a growing industrial town whose population of nearly 9,000 was torn by tension and bitter resentments."[1] Braddock was a magnet like Silicon Valley is today because steel was a growth industry that filled the newspapers with stories of success.

The reality was a bit different as described by historian, William Serrin: "The myth of the steel millionaire also seduced the people of the steel towns. Carnegie, Frick, Schwab, Julian Kennedy, Alva Dinkey, William E. Corey and his brother A. A. Corey, William Dickson, A. R. Hunt—they and others started poor and became rich, important men. They were regarded as representatives of that quintessential American hero, the self-made man, and were much honored by the townspeople. Many a mill-town boy, especially in the early days, went into the mill with the hope of making himself rich, a big man in steel, even though it was impossible in most cases to rise from the rank and file. Finally, the sheer size of the mill, the gigantic machines, the vast sheds, the high cauldrons of bubbling steel, overwhelmed the men who worked there. Men could not work in such a setting and regard themselves as important."[2] Braddock was like a gold rush mining town with a few making millions while thousands would find only disappointment.

Residents said the sun rose at 10 a.m. and set at 2 p.m. The smoke and iron dust lingered everywhere. The additional gray of an afternoon thunderstorm could make it as dark as night at midday. There were no streetlights when Schwab arrived but the Bessemers provided an orange, dull lighting. Streets were dirty and muddy. Iron dust was constantly in the air. The women had to continuously wash to try to keep up but it was a losing battle. In the spring floods were common. Most residents lived more like tenant farmers than city folk. People raised chickens and pigs and gardened to supplement their

---

[1] Hessen, 13
[2] Serrin, 166

tables. McDevitt's was the main store near the entrance to Edgar Thomson. McDevitt's was a grocery store and dry goods "emporium." It was a three-story brick building. The ground floor was the store and the upper floors housed five clerks. Schwab started as a clerk at McDevitt's store. It was also at McDevitt's that Schwab first met Bill Jones.

While I have focused on the Carnegie's "boys of Braddock," there were others who formed rival steel operations via Braddock. Another famous boy who got his start as a clerk also in Braddock was Ernest Tener Weir. Pittsburgh-born Weir started as a clerk at Braddock Wire in 1890. He learned the wire and steel business, progressing up in management. By 1908, he was a millionaire owner/operator of over ten wire and plate mills. In 1910 he started a new mill and town in West Virginia. That city is today, Weirton, West Virginia, and the company is Weirton Steel. Weirton is on the Ohio River about forty miles from Pittsburgh; it looks and has a similar history to that of Braddock.

Braddock Wire would ultimately become part of United States Steel. It too, however, is a story of yet another boy attracted to Braddock. The founder of Braddock Wire in the 1880s was Wallace Rowe. Rowe was born in St. Louis and started working there at a small wire company. St. Louis was a poor location for wire making because of the distance of the mills and labor costs. Rowe and his associates started a nationwide search for a better location. Braddock stood out for its closeness to the steel sources, its railroad connections to the west (barbed wire was a big product) and cheap and available labor (the plant had over 1,200 employees at its peak). In a few years Braddock Wire merged with Consolidated Steel of Chicago with Rowe in charge. Rowe, a close student of Carnegie, believed in economy of scale and continued to buy and merge other companies. By 1901, as American Steel and Wire it was by far the largest wire manufacturer in the United

States. In 1901 United States Steel absorbed it, creating another Braddock millionaire. All of these steel related businesses in Braddock caused even a bigger wave of immigrants.

Tension with the Hungarian and Slav immigrants in Braddock started in the late 1880s when Henry Clay Frick decided to bring them in as a strategy of lower wages for mill laborers. Author David McCullough noted the tension: "The steel bosses, like Henry Clay Frick, had been bringing them in by the thousands to work in Braddock and Homestead. They were single men mostly, willing to work for the lowest wages, and under the worst conditions, just to save enough to go back home and buy a small farm on the Danube. They got the toughest jobs, worked hard, and were generally hated by the Irish, the German, and American workers."[3] This hard work under hot, dangerous conditions had earned the respect of Braddock's Bill Jones.

Still there was a great deal of dislike for the Southern European immigrants. Schwab biographer Robert Hesson described the distrust: "The 'native stock' of Braddock, descendants of the settlers from England, Ireland, and Scotland, feared the growing influx of 'foreign' laborers, most of whom were Italians, Slavs, and Hungarians. The Irish in particular, did not mix with the Slavs, Hungarians and Italians. The Irish grouped all the Southern Europeans as "Hunkies." The Irish maintained their own bars and eating-places. These Southern European men, the unskilled workers, at the Edgar Thomson Works, were regarded as vulgar, ignorant, unclean, ruthless, and degenerate 'foreigners.'" The Hungarians and Slavs with a few Italians lived near the river in "Hunkietown." Living conditions were extremely poor with no running water. This overcrowded poor area became Braddock's "First Ward."

---

[3] McCullough, 175

While Braddock offered career paths for most, "In the great school of steel-making, the lower grades are filled entirely with pupils who can never be promoted. The Huns, Slavs, Finns, and Italians who form the main body of the workers never rise above the position of common labourers, except in the most unusual instances. They have hands but no heads. Among them are no embryonic Schwabs or Coreys." Ultimately the practice would end decades later in a management ceiling against Catholics in general. This dual application of the exceptional motivational theories of Carnegie would be the source of unionization and labor problems. It was also at the heart of failure of the unions in Braddock. The Irish in particular refused to come into the Amalgamated Steelworkers because of the Hungarians and Slavs. The Irish tended to prefer the secret organizations and the social lodges that formed an informal union with management. Jobs were handled through a "good old boy" network with the foremen and bosses. Jones and Schwab had a broader vision, in which all employees could prosper on their own merit.

In the 1890s the nature of the town was changing. A small influx of Irish continued but the main influx was the Austrians and Hungarians. On the census records Austrians increased to about 20% or about the total of the Irish at 24%. Hungarians were at about 19% of the population by the turn of the century. In Europe, the Austrians and the Hungarians were artificially united in the Austro-Hungarian Empire. These, however, were distinctly different people. The Austrians were Germans, in language and culture. The census numbers are confusing because of the nature of the census. A Slovenian, Pole, Serbian, Croat, or Czech may have listed himself or herself as Austrian. "Hungarians" included Slovaks, Croatians, and Serbians. The majority of these Eastern Europeans were located in the "First Ward" and Hunkietown. The language of the street in these areas was Slovak. The 1910 census showed that the largest number of foreign-born residents in North Braddock and Braddock were from Austria. (The "native" Braddock residents remained in control). Records of 1910 show almost all of Europe represented in the population including France, Sweden, Denmark, Switzerland and Belgium. The Irish, Scots, Welsh and Germans still controlled the town politically until at least the 1920s.

Ethnic divisions among the native residents and Southern European groups were very well defined. The various groups had their own churches and social clubs. For example the Croatians went to the Croatian Beneficial Club and the Italians had the Dante Club. These clubs offered recreation and dancing and ethnic music. Churches followed the same pattern, offering services in the native languages and observing traditional customs. While the majority of the population after 1880 was Catholic, there were differences even here. The Hungarians belonged to the Byzantine sect of the Catholic Church. While the Byzantine rite was in communion with the Pope, it was a uniquely orthodox rite. The Slavs tended to be Roman Catholic, which further distinguished them from their national grouping with the Hungarians. After time a number of "lost" Catholic Hungarians started to join Protestant sects. In 1890, there was even a Baptist Hungarian Church in Braddock. At times between 1880 and 1920, there were as many as ten different Catholic churches each servicing a particular ethnic group. The ethnic clubs also acted as employment and social agencies for the new immigrant.

The Austrians tended to blend in the best with the natives because they were less likely to form up as a strong ethnic group. The Austrians had been the first of the non-native residents. Their strategy was to assimilate into the native white groups and avoid becoming a distinct ethnic group. The

Austrians tied in well also with their German brothers since they shared a language. The Austrians mixed well with the native Irish as well.

Many historians have seen that these poor Southern European immigrants created a culture stronger and more distinct than they had in Europe. Historian John Bodnar described it: "Confined in lower-level occupations in the steel plant, housed in separate row homes, unable to rise occupationally, subject to economic vicissitudes, and lacking positions of power in the steel town, the newcomers turned inward. Croats, Serbs, Slovenes, Bulgarians, and Blacks displayed almost no regard for Anglo-Saxon concerns such as civic reform or local politics. Immigrants had to deal with problems, which concerned their own congregations, homelands, and ultimately their own identities. Unsure of their status in a new land and faced with rejection and criticism from the old stock, they debated issues that were peculiar to their own ethnic communities. And in the process, they acquired a new ethnic consciousness which surpassed anything they had known in Europe."[4] They developed unique rituals and customs to fit their new environment. They held on to their native language for use at church and social events well into the twentieth century with strong remnants even existing today.

There was a very small population of Blacks and Mexicans brought in at times to replace strikers. Because of Braddock's hold as a mill town, fewer Blacks were used compared to neighboring towns such as McKeesport and Homestead. In general the Blacks even had it worse than the "Hunkies" in the furnaces, working in the coke works. The coke works were filled with toxic fumes that considerably reduced the life span of workers. Blacks had no hope whatsoever of advancement.

---

[4] Hoerr, 171

The mill changed the nature of the town forever. The mill ran twenty-four hours a day, seven days a week. There were major working shifts at six o'clock in the morning and six o'clock in the evening. When the mill operated on three shift changes, there was a change at two o'clock in the afternoon. It was really a town that never slept. This schedule was a seven-day a week routine, including holidays, as the mill ran by nature continuously. Bars, restaurants, stores and some businesses were open all around the clock. Some of the ethnic clubs were also open all night. Life tended to revolve around the mill schedule. Funerals were held in the homes. The house was open 24 hours for the different shifts to pay their respects. The women cooked large meals every 8 to 10 hours to feed visitors coming off the shifts to pay respects. Sadly, this was a common occurrence. Fatal accidents in the mill were a weekly event and every family could talk of a relative who died in the mills.

Time for social events was extremely limited for the workers. The twelve-hour, seven-day week was oppressive. Holidays were just another working day. Relaxation amounted to a few hours in the saloons.

Probably a side note is needed here for those unfamiliar with steel mills. A blast furnace runs twenty-four hours a day, seven days a week. Usually a blast furnace of the time might run for years until it was taken down to reline the refractory brick, which is eventually eroded away by the process and the heat. A blast furnace could be "banked" as it was called, for a number of days, but it was a risky proposition. The danger in "banking" was that the furnace would bridge or freeze up. If the furnace froze it required a major rebuild. It is always best even today to run a blast furnace as a continuous operation. There was only one time in over a hundred twenty years that a blast furnace wasn't running in the Monongahela valley; that was in the great steel depression of the 1980s.

Having worked in the mills for over twenty years, one of the best descriptions of inside the mill of the 1880s is that of Thomas Bell in his novel of Braddock, *Out of this Furnace:* "On clear nights, with the first taste of spring in the air, there were few stars visible once he was inside the mill. Looking up he saw the furnaces and stoves, piled one behind the other into the distance, small lights, and over beyond the rail mill the wavering glow of the Bessemers. A steel mill at night made a man feel small as he trudged into its pile of structures, its shadows. A cast-house filled suddenly with illumination as the furnace was tapped and the bright glare of the molten metal was like a conflagration around the end of an alleyway, silhouetting waiting ladles, the corner of an engine house, skeleton beams. Smoke swirled lazily through angular shadows. Passing, he felt the heat of the ladles; up in the cast-house hardly more of the men than their faces could be seen across the metal's glare. The dinkey's engineer sat motionless in the cab, thinking his own thoughts."[5]

Braddock historian George Lamb, gives a vivid description of the town outside the mill: "With this element, and every other house on Braddock Avenue a saloon, running full blast twenty-four hours a day, Braddock had much the aspect of a western Mining Camp. Women seldom went on Braddock Avenue on Saturday nights. Street fighting seemed to be a favorite and universal diversion." Nationality gangs formed as well and added to the fighting. The population was probably over 70% or more single in the 1880s. Another historian looked at this way: "Meanwhile, alone in an inhospitable town, they sought pleasure mainly at Braddock's bars and brothels—or so it seemed to the natives." The managers and superintendents stayed away from the saloons and bars of the workingmen. Managers started to live further up the hill into

---

[5] Thomas Bell, *Out of this Furnace* (University of Pittsburgh Press: Pittsburgh, 1976), 163

North Braddock. A restaurant on Braddock Avenue known as the "old McKinney Club House" served as a meeting place for management for lunch and after work. McKinney's was torn down in 1912 to make room for the new open-hearth shop.

In the 1890s the town stabilized a bit. Immigrants from Europe were coming to stay. Housing was being developed, even if poorly. "Hunkietown" and the "First Ward" were the worst of the housing. Originally the First Ward was Irish but as the new immigrants poured in; the Irish held the higher paying jobs and started to move up the hill. Some of the Irish remained in the First Ward as saloon owners. The houses of the First Ward were close wooden and cinder brick homes. Between the groupings of houses was a court area where water could be pumped and a toilet maintained. It also was a meeting place for the women during the day. On weekends the courts were places of social card games, eating and recreation. The houses were unbelievably hot and oppressive in the summer and drafty in the winter. One room in these houses held two to four families. The First Ward of old is mostly gone having been appropriated by Edgar Thomson Works.

Housing was at its worst in the First Ward near the mill. This is where immigrants entered Braddock's society. Moving up in society meant moving up the "hill." Skilled workers and front line supervision earned enough to move further up the hill. Wealthier residents tended to move up the hill into North Braddock. Further up into the hills you found a class of poor farmers and miners. One way to progress up the hill was to become involved in the local rackets. Gambling was a major type of recreation and the cash flow was enormous. The Irish were the first "mob" to control gambling and the rackets.

The 1890s brought the emergence of the streetcar or light electric railways. The first electric railway in Braddock was the Braddock and Turtle Creek Railway in 1891. The original cars were horse drawn cars from New York, which were converted to electric power. The Mellon brothers (Mellon Banking) purchased the then called Braddock Electric Company in 1896. This Mellon company was the Monongahela Street Railway Company. Prior to the Mellon brothers, the company served Braddock and North Braddock. Monongahela Street Railways opened up the "Yellow Line" connecting Braddock and Homestead via the West Braddock Bridge in 1897. This connected families and the two great mills of Carnegie. Through mergers, a new company again emerged: Pittsburgh Railways Company in 1902. For five cents the streetcars connected the great mills of the Monongahela valley to the town of Braddock. It is estimated that 40,000 men in the valley were carried to work and back daily. It is fascinating that these very workers supplied most of the country light rails for the streetcars to run on.

By the 1900s second generation Slovaks, Austrians and others were moving up the hill by becoming small business owners. Many of these had started as bartenders and store employees. In addition to mill employees, there was a growing group of white middle class professionals such as lawyers, which lived in North Braddock. This group was very biased and did not associate with "mill workers" including low and middle managers. They tended to form country clubs in the surrounding areas.

One of the favorite rackets was the "numbers" which was a local run lottery. The numbers were extremely popular and made many a rich Irishman. Saloons and stores served as fronts for number writing. This brought in a small Jewish element into the rackets. Actually there was a small Jewish population in Braddock and Rankin during the 1880s. Most of these were Slovak immigrant Jews. There was even a synagogue in Rankin. The Jews tended to run the small stores and retailing firms and some of the rackets.

There was a minor amount of "organized" bootlegging. Generally, however, the Eastern Europeans ran stills to supply booze for social events and Saturday night card games. Saloons were still popular because they offered an escape from the mill and dirt. Saloons and bars increased in density as you approached the mill entrance. Workers could purchase a monthly contract to have the bar set up a shot of whiskey and beer that could be drunk quickly prior to entering the mill. This combination was called a "puddler and helper." This is the origin of the "shot and beer" so popular in the Braddock area.

With the ethnic immigration came the mythical residents of Braddock. The oldest of these is the hero of Scots-Irish immigrants, Mike Fink. Some believed he was born on the Monongahela at Braddock lock #2 or Port Perry in the 1770s. The first written tales of Mike Fink appeared in the 1820s. He became a national folk hero of riverboat workers on the Ohio, Monongahela, Mississippi and others. By legend he lived in western Pennsylvania, New Orleans and St. Louis, finally dying in a Rocky mountain gunfight.

Another mythical resident of Braddock was the "steel angel" known as Tubal-Cain. This appears to be an Austrian legend that a guardian angel was assigned to the Braddock from the beginning of the world. Tubal-Cain was said to account for the many lucky events in the development of the steel industry at Braddock. It was Tubal-Cain, which was the spirit the Indians saw protecting George Washington at the battle of Braddock's Field. It was Tubal-Cain that brought Carnegie and Schwab to Braddock. Tubal-Cain was the spirit that has saved Edgar Thomson Works over and over again from extinction.

The "real" mythical Braddock hero is Joe Magarac. Magarac was a mythical gigantic steelworker. Magarac worked a twelve-hour shift in the Edgar Thomas Works and another at Homestead every day. He is believed to have been born in a mountain of ore and rode the rails to Braddock. He worked in Edgar Thomson Works squeezing out rails from molten steel. He was known to be a good friend of John Henry, who came to Braddock to get Magarac's rails. Mill stories of the great man appearing late at night out at the 50-ton furnaces were common. When there was trouble is when Joe would materialize. He loved to mingle with the workers on the night shift.

Joe's nationality is debatable. The Hungarians claim him as well as Croatians. Both ethnic groups say the word Magarac means "jackass." Some claim he is modeled after a real Croatian steelworker known as Mestrovic, which is a Croatian name and appears in many of the published stories of Joe Magarac. The nationality debate goes to the search for the origin of the legend as well. The popularity of the legend with the early Croatian immigrants of Rankin suggests a Croatian origin. Others claim its origin is over a hundred years old in the Hungarian population. In any case the story of Joe Magarac was well established by the 1930s. National fame of this Braddock resident came with the published account of folklorist, Owen Francis, in a 1931 *Scribner's Magazine* article. In the 1960s, Irwin Sharpo in *Heroes in American Folklore* published the best story of Joe Magarac. Joe had a revival of interest in the 1970s when he appeared in the advertising campaigns of *Iron City Beer.*

With the decline of steel in the Monongahela valley, Joe is believed to be sleeping or too weak to materialize. Some say he haunts the old Carrie furnaces in Rankin. One of the legends has Joe resting in Braddock's cemetery with his boss, Bill Jones. Another legend I got first hand from an old steel worker is that Joe lies sleeping on a high hill in North Braddock, that being the highest point in Allegheny county with the best view of the Monongahela valley. He watches the valley, awaiting the return of big steel. Legend has it that some future Braddock steel maker will awake him. Joe is immortalized in the stained glass window at Pittsburgh's international headquarters of the United Steelworkers of America.

One of the great landmarks of Braddock is the Braddock Carnegie Library. Built in 1889 by Carnegie it was his first in the United States but second in the world. Carnegie had built his first library in his hometown of Dunfermline, Scotland in 1881. Carnegie built the library in Braddock as a community center for the men of Edgar Thomson Works. The complex contained a bowling alley, swimming pool and music hall (1893 addition). The music hall included a pipe organ, oak seats and paneling as well as skylights. The library also contained some of the original artifacts of the Battle of Braddock found during the building of Edgar Thomson Works. In 1900, Carnegie made a further gift of a "Winged Mercury" statue, which was a bronze reproduction of a 1574 statue by Florentine sculptor, Giam Bologna. Carnegie's heart was in the right place but for the majority of Braddock workers, more basic needs were not being addressed. Ethnic centers played a much bigger role in the life of workers. The library would, however, benefit later generations like myself.

One failed socialistic effort of Carnegie in Braddock was the Braddock Cooperative Society. Carnegie offered the building rent-free to the employees but insisted that the men manage it themselves. Carnegie had hoped that this would teach a form of practical economics to the men. The company through the cooperative did supply coal for heating at half the cost of free market distributors. Still the cooperative store lacked the variety and service of free market stores and ultimately failed. The store had been one of the general community improvements that Bill Jones believed critical to satisfy the workforce. Jones had started another type of mill socialism that of employment agency. Working with the local "lodges," a good worker could assure the employment of his sons in the mill. Injured workers were also given office-type work where possible. The good paying work of the mills tended to keep families and generations together in Braddock and reinforced the strong ethnic flavor of the Monongahela valley for decades.

Carnegie biographer Peter Krass describes Braddock today: "Today, the Edgar Thomson steel mill is the sole survivor of the Carnegie mills along the Monongahela River; the others have been razed. Its hometown of Braddock remains bleak, however; many shops on the main street are boarded up, and the town is empty of spirit. The stark contrast between the desolate streets of Braddock and the vitality discovered in Carnegie's libraries best symbolize the great contradictions of Carnegie himself."[6] Braddock awaits the awakening by a future Braddock steel maker of Joe Magarac that the legend promises.

---

[6] Krass, 541

Chapter 9

"The careers of Schwab, Corey, Dinkey, and Dickson were classic examples of the American 'self-made-man' success story."
–*Gerald Eggert, 1981*

The Boys of Braddock

The "boys of Braddock" were the core of the Carnegie Veterans Association, which met as a group into the late 1930s. The Carnegie Veterans Association was not a literary group, but a group bound by heritage, philosophy and purpose. The organization actually had a charter and mission. The Carnegie Veterans Association held annual meetings at Carnegie's New York home and Carnegie and his wife often attended. One of the boys described the group: "While we were all leading the strenuous life with the Carnegie Co. in the old partnership days, we were usually worried and cumbered with many cares, and often our zeal led us to do and say things which to an outsider would have seemed rude, but no outsider knew or could know the feeling of loyalty and kinship which existed between us all. We were one family in the sense of each one striving to make himself the most important member, and ready to defend all the rest against any charge from the outside, whether fair or unfair. Those days were to us all, an education along lines which always bring success and whose value will remain with us for life."[1] They communicated with each other over the years exchanging views and helping each other. In cities such as New York and Pittsburgh, the members met routinely for lunch. Many of them would team up in other organizations and in the founding of new companies.

---

[1] Eggert, 19

It was a group that looked to Carnegie and Bill Jones as idols. They were also known as Carnegie's "young geniuses." They are tied to Braddock in some cases by birth and marriage as well as starting at Edgar Thomson Works, but always in spirit and management beliefs. Their monument was Edgar Thomson Works. They were Industrial Edwardians, more progressive than their employers. They are the heart of the American Industrial Revolution. They represented a management style believing in motivation, technology, and most of all the basic drives of people. They had their weaknesses as a group as well. As a group they believed unionism would fail to represent the worker in the long run.

They are represented by:

    Bill Jones
    Charles Schwab
    Alva Dinkey
    Julian Kennedy
    William Corey
    James Gayley
    Ambrose Monell
    William Dickson
    David Kerr
    Thomas Morrison
    Joe Schwab

But there are others less known and lost to history. We must also include mythical members such as Joe Magarac.

The "boys of Braddock" were ex-Edgar Thomson veterans and managers. Charles Schwab and Julian Kennedy, were the real creators of the new massive steel trust. The "boys" would go out to change the steel industry and American industry. They would bring Bill Jones's belief in the eight-hour day to reality. They would pioneer an experimental approach to fairness in the workplace. They would implement an industrial safety model for all of industry. It would be the boys who first brought in production planning, metallurgical and research departments. They would make the United States a world leader in armor, shipbuilding and armaments which would assure victories in two world wars. In World War II, the boys' Monongahela valley would make more steel than Nazi Germany and Imperial Japan.

The formation of United States Steel ended the golden years for the boys of Braddock. Still the most productive years were ahead of them. Schwab headed USS Corporation with four of "the boys of Braddock" at his side. The men of Bill Jones had now become the leadership of the world's largest company. For most, however, their careers where just beginning to blossom. The first vice-president of United States Steel at Schwab's right hand was Edgar Thomson veteran, James Gayley. "Second" vice-president was Schwab man at Homestead (Swissvale born), William Brown Dickson. Boyhood friend, William Corey was also a Vice-President at Schwab's side. Braddock boy Alva Dinkey was President of the largest division of USS Corporation-Carnegie Steel.

James Gayley was a graduate of Lafayette College in Mining and Metallurgical Engineering. He had started his career under Bill Jones as Superintendent of the Edgar Thomson blast furnaces. In fact, Gayley had ties with Jones going back to Crane Iron Works in Jones's hometown of Catasauqua, Pennsylvania. He was a brilliant innovator and inventor. His inventions of bronze cooling plating and dry blast at the furnaces had almost doubled the output. Carnegie had always included Gayley in his "young geniuses." When Charles Schwab took a short leave from USS in 1902, Schwab noted: "Steel company's affairs will move without any hitch. Mr. Gayley is quite capable of attending to all my duties. All my organization [Carnegie Veterans] are loyal and energetic and will do their best—will in fact try harder than if I were here."[2]

Gayley was indeed a great manager. He had followed Schwab in taking over the administration of Edgar Thomson when Schwab returned to Homestead in 1892. As blast furnace superintendent, Gayley had been extremely popular being an Irishman. He had trained under the world famous other boy of Braddock, Julian Kennedy. He had been at Jones's side the night of his death in the furnaces. He had stood with Schwab in the New Year's Eve uprising at Edgar Thomson Works. He was known as the "pig iron king."

Gayley was extremely active in the running of the Carnegie Library of Braddock, bringing in national speakers. He believed like Schwab in the technical training of the workers. Language training in English was also offered at the library. Gayley's wife was also active in the running of library programs for steelworkers' wives. Gayley's wife and Corey's wife were extremely active in the building of Braddock Hospital.

Gayley's boss and furnace mentor, Julian Kennedy, had been another of the "boys." Kennedy was the best educated of the boys having studied metallurgy and chemistry at Yale. Kennedy had started his career at the Brier Hill Steel Company in Youngstown, Ohio. Kennedy had come to Braddock in 1878, to build Edgar Thomson's first blast furnace under Bill Jones. Starting with an old charcoal furnace wreck, within three years the blast furnaces of Edgar Thomson were known throughout the world. Carnegie then moved him to Lucy Furnaces and again Kennedy achieved new world furnace output records. In 1886, Kennedy came to Homestead to build the massive open-hearth shop. Kennedy became known for his application of preventive maintenance long before its popularity. In one of the few known Kennedy

---

[2] Hessen, 140

quotes, he said, "The Superintendent who repairs on the same lines as last time, without seeing his way to improve, to strengthen and to make more effective his furnace; we have no use for that class of man." In 1890, Kennedy became a consulting steel engineer for J. P. Morgan and was instrumental in the formation of United States Steel. In 1906, it would be on Kennedy review that Tennessee Coal and Iron was added to the United States Steel Corporation. This was a huge addition to USS in terms of ore and mining. Finally, Kennedy would recommend the purchase of Clairton Steel for USS, which would give USS ownership of the greatest steel valley ever. Julian Kennedy was the Carnegie veteran who built the Monongahela valley into the center of world steel production, having been involved with blast furnaces at Lucy Furnaces, Edgar Thomson Works, Carrie Furnaces and Duquesne as well as open-hearths at Homestead and Edgar Thomson. In the 1920s Julian and his brother built the first integrated steel mills in China and India.

The Monongahela valley consisted of Clairton, Duquesne, Carrie Furnaces, Edgar Thomson and Homestead. Not even the Ruhr valley of Germany could come close to this steel mega valley. In fact for many years the output of the Monongahela valley would out-produce the whole country of Germany. More steel has been produced in that ten-mile valley than any other similar spot in the world. It's hard to imagine such a great industrial valley will ever rise again. This was the greatest tribute to the "boys of Braddock."

Another of the boys was William Corey. Corey as we have seen came from one of the oldest Braddock families. He was a friend of Schwab. Corey was four years younger than Schwab but Schwab was his older "brother." When Schwab was working as a clerk, Corey was mining coal on back shifts. He had started a few years after Schwab in Edgar Thomson's chemical laboratory. He didn't rise at the fast pace of Schwab but he gained more hands-on experience. At night Corey took business courses at Duff's Business College in Pittsburgh. Like Schwab, Corey studied chemistry and metallurgy on his own, becoming an expert in them. Corey was a tireless student. He particularly excelled in his study of metallurgy. As Superintendent of Homestead's armor department, Corey would develop and patent a line of steel alloys and hardening practices. Corey's armor was famous even in Krupp's Germany.

Historians give Corey a mixed review. Casson, author of *Romance of Steel,* said, "Corey is reserved, stern-faced, non-magnetic." While Serrin, author of *Homestead,* said, "The workers liked him and so did many fellow executives." Part of this is that he lacked the smiling personality of Schwab. He was reserved and somewhat of a loner. This caused him problems with the press as well as historians. The press dubbed him the "Iron Chancellor" because of his secretive behavior. Corey was not able to put Homestead behind him, as was Schwab. Schwab was a hard man to emulate; he had the perfect balance of organization and individual. Corey always had Schwab's and Carnegie's support throughout his career.

Corey, however, had the virtues of the "boys." He was goal driven, a motivator, persistent, and loyal. Corey had moved to Homestead as the superintendent of the plate mill. Eventually he became superintendent of the armor department. This was the ideal position for him because of his expertise in metallurgical engineering. Armor was the most complex product chemically and metallurgically being produced at the time. Unfortunately he was there for the 1892 strike, which would mark all the managers. When Schwab became president of Carnegie Steel, William Corey followed him as general superintendent of Homestead. He ran Homestead very effectively but he was never to be popular with the union.

As general superintendent of Homestead, Corey was instrumental in the development of the metallurgical and quality control departments. He worked with Schwab in getting the University of Pittsburgh to start a metallurgical engineering degree program. One of those metallurgists from the University of Pittsburgh came to Homestead in the 1890s, Robert Brown Carnahan. Carnahan became an open-hearth expert and would go on to help form Armco Steel in Ohio.

Corey, after the resignation of Schwab as president of United States Steel Corporation, followed as president in 1903. When Corey became president of USS, another Braddock boy, Charles Dickson became first vice-president of USS. In 1909, David Kerr, Corey's fellow Edgar Thomson laboratory boy rose to a vice-president of USS. Corey, like Schwab, struggled with USS's chairman, Judge Elbert Gary. Corey made some social mistakes but to Gary they were far beyond those of Schwab's gambling. Corey got involved with a showgirl and decided to divorce his Braddock wife. Worse, he had a flashy New York wedding. Ultimately Corey would show his independence like Schwab, and Gary forced him to resign in 1911. With the resignation of Corey and the prior ones of Schwab, Dinkey and Gayley, United States Steel was no longer the corporation of the boys but of Morgan and Gary.

Corey, like the majority of the boys, held that unions had no place in the steel industry. At his retirement dinner in 1911 he summarized his view: "If there has been any one subject in which I have been intensely interested, it is that of what I am pleased to call 'free labor' as against so-called 'union labor.' The Company in which I passed the early years of my business life had to face this question many times, and decided once and for all in 1892 that however beautiful in theory, as a matter of practical operation the intervention of any third party between a company and its employees could not be tolerated. No sane man will tolerate the abstract right of the workingman to organize. It is the 'condition, however, and not a theory that confronts us.' Until organized labor has demonstrated its ability to deal with economic problems in an enlightened way and progressive spirit, and abandons its reactionary attitude, as indicated by its pernicious practices of restriction of output, dead level of wages regardless of efficiency, and closed shop, we must deal with hindrance to progress and steadfastly refuse to be hampered by its unreasonable demands."

Four of "the boys of Braddock," Jones, Schwab, Corey and Gayley, held strongly to this line of no unions. It appears to have been colored by the blood-stained glasses of Homestead. Just as important was their Edgar Thomson Works experience, which showed that with enlightened management, steel production could run smoothly without a union. It was clearly the view of their boss, Carnegie. Carnegie's view on labor was summarized in an 1886 magazine article: "*First.* That compensation is paid the men based upon a sliding scale in proportion to the prices received for the product. *Second.* A proper organization of the men of every works to be made, by which the natural leaders, the best men, will eventually come to the front and confer freely with the employers. *Third.* Peaceful arbitration to be in all cases resorted to for settlement of differences which the owners and mill committee cannot themselves adjust. *Fourth.* No interruption ever to occur in the operations."[3] The labor policy of the boys followed Carnegie's ideas with the exception of the sliding scale.

Carnegie and the "boys" had the Victorian view of the employer as a father of a family. This paternal approach was a fair approach but demanded absolute loyalty. The paternal approach assumed the employer knew what the men needed and would supply those needs. The boys took this basic view and developed a more progressive Edwardian management

---

[3] George Swetnam, *Andrew Carnegie* (Boston: Twayne Publishers, 1980), 92

style. Wages were very much like a generous allowance to the "sons" of the company. If the employer was taking in less money, his loyal sons were expected to understand a reduction in allowance for the good of the family. Carnegie and Jones, like Morrell at Cambria before them, believed in helping the men buy houses and food. Carnegie actually believed that in general, most management abused American labor. In Carnegie's speech on the state of labor: "I am certain that disputes about wages do not account for one half the disagreements between capital and labor. There is lack of due appreciation and of kind treatment of employees upon the part of employers."[4]

There is no doubt that Carnegie and the boys cared about the employees. The "anti-union" approach of the core group of the boys was not anti-labor. Carnegie cared, but in those paternal ways that were not well understood. One of the reasons that this book could be written is directly attributable to Carnegie. As a boy, I loved the Carnegie libraries. My earliest escapes were in the Swissvale Carnegie Library but I soon learned of what I still consider one of the world's greatest library/museum complexes, that of the Carnegie Library in Pittsburgh's Oakland Library of Carnegie. These libraries were great gifts to the communities. Recently Pittsburgh was listed in the top ten of U.S. cities in higher education degrees. I believe this is directly attributable to the great Carnegie Libraries of the area. In the end Carnegie donated over 3,000 libraries worldwide, 4,100 church organs, founded universities and established many funds. He differed from his fellow robber barons, like Vanderbilt and Rockefeller, in that he refused to pass on his millions for future generations, which Carnegie considered a disgrace. He left enough for his immediate family to live out their lives in comfort. He firmly believed that starting youth out with

---

[4] Carnegie, 244

money would destroy them. When his great-grandson visited Braddock in the 1970s, he had to save money for a year to make the trip!

Historians miss the point in the characters of Carnegie, Jones and Schwab. Historians see contradictions and hypocritical views within them. They miss the real consistency in them. The considered themselves, like the historical heroes they loved, men of destiny. They were fathers for the mills they ran and the creators of communities. To their credit they considered themselves trusted stewards of the money God had blessed them with. It was a mental Utopia that was their model. It was as Carnegie titled one of his books, *The Gospel of Wealth*. It was a consistent theory that was embraced by this group of industrialists. Their views were also based on their experiences and beliefs. They were men who did not work for money as we have seen. They worked for achievement. They assumed this was basic to human nature. In light of modern philosophy, they were only partially right in just a generalization.

The paternal approach, however, is difficult to apply in practice. To be successful with such an approach requires the people-oriented personalities such as those of Carnegie, Schwab and Jones. Other boys such as Corey never could master the technique. Yet, amazingly, it would be another branch of the boys (Dinkey and Dickson) that would revolutionize the American approach towards labor.

Another fault of the labor theory of the boys arose from the dual application of their theory. The ability to rise quickly based on merit and drive was basic to the theory of the boys. The weaknesses of the Industrial Victorians, such as Carnegie and especially Frick, were that a different set of rules applied for the Hungarians, Slavs and Italians. This group did not have that opportunity. It was in this group that the labor problems, as well as the union, first arose. Bill Jones had tried to unsuccessfully change this because he perceived its problems and the future roots of unionism.

Corey's right-hand man, and one of the "boys," was to become a leader in labor management. That man was William Brown Dickson. Like Bill Jones honed Charles Schwab, Schwab honed Dickson. Dickson was born in Braddock's neighbor town, Swissvale. He had the wealthiest start of the boys, being that his father, Charles E. Dickson, owned a Braddock and Swissvale coal company. That company had also operated lime kilns in Braddock on the East hills above the Sixth Street ravine in Braddock. He started his career as a "Pulpit Boy Crane Operator" at the Homestead works. He moved to mill clerk for a number of years. As a mill clerk, he worked days and went to night school at Duff's Business College in Pittsburgh. It was a tiring schedule but he learned record keeping in the classroom and on the job. During this time he lived across river in Swissvale, crossing the Monongahela each day in a rowboat.

In the disorder at times at Homestead, Dickson made his mark by improving customer deliveries by better production planning. Mill productivity was the religion of Carnegie steel mills. Superintendents, looking for more production records, tended to run the large repeating orders moving smaller orders down the schedule. Inventories clogged the mills and missed deliveries were routine. Management in the Order and Shipping Department suffered from burn-out in an impossible task. Dickson worked out a system of setting schedules to optimize both production and delivery. This is where his studies at night business school paid off. Dickson's system actually resulted in what Schwab and Carnegie called the "operating department." This department was the model for future production planning departments throughout American industry. It stands with industrial chemistry as another pioneering field developed by the "boys of Braddock."

In his studies of production planning and input, Dickson included the theories of the students of Braddock's Bill Jones; Dickson became convinced that the twelve-hour day and the seven-day workweek actually were detrimental to productivity. Dickson called them the "twin relics of barbarism." Later Dickson would take on the leadership of American industry in labor reform. Dickson was also a man of arts and writing. He wrote serious poetry and essays. Like Schwab and so many of the boys he was an extraordinary reader. One biographer noted: "Raised as a child to love and respect good literature, Dickson began to buy books at the age of nine. Now, however, he assembled a large library, which he used constantly. The range and quality of his reading—from the classics to the most recent writers—gave him greater polish and erudition than many of his college-educated contemporaries. Dickson was forever copying poems and ideas from books he read, weaving them into his conversations, correspondence, and public addresses."[5]

As a personal note I have always felt the closest to Dickson. I lived most of my own childhood within a few blocks of where Dickson did in Swissvale. I know well the part of the Monongahela where he launched his rowboat every day. I well remember the challenges of working in mill management in the day and going to Pittsburgh night school. I respect his pioneering views on labor management. His production planning approach was one I favored in my steel career. We both have that love of reading and writing. Where Carnegie and Schwab loved literature and mill management, they tended to put them in separate boxes. Dickson found a way to blend them.

When Schwab moved from General Superintendent of Homestead to President of Carnegie Steel, Dickson moved to special secretary. Dickson functioned as secretary to Schwab's

---

[5] Eggert, 27

famous Saturday operating meetings of the various Pittsburgh operations. He was stationed in New York so he could summarize the meeting and Pittsburgh operations for Carnegie at his New York headquarters. In 1899, Carnegie made him a junior partner (in effect a sure millionaire). In 1900 he became Schwab's assistant as President of Carnegie Steel. With the formation of United States Steel, he became one of Schwab's vice-presidents.

Alva Dinkey was one the more moderate of the boys. Alva was a Braddock boy, who started as a water boy at Edgar Thomson Works. Dinkey was, of course, both a boyhood friend and brother-in-law of Charles Schwab. The young Dinkey was remembered by Braddock steelworkers as: "A bright, round-faced boy who carried water for the furnace men and was always asking questions. At sixteen he learned telegraphy at a little station near Braddock. Then he began at the bottom of the ladder in the machine shop, worked his way up and left to learn the trade of an electrician. Every change meant a drop in wages, but a gain in knowledge. Entering the Homestead works as a clerk, he introduced electrical machinery on a large scale. At twenty-six he became general superintendent of Homestead, with ten thousand men under his career."[6] This moving around to learn was a key career strategy of the "boys of Braddock."

Dinkey ultimately followed Corey to become the general superintendent at Homestead in 1901, as Corey had followed Schwab. Finally, Dinkey would rise to president of Carnegie Steel (as part of USS) in 1903. Dinkey learned skills as a telegraph operator and electrician in Braddock that left a mark on the town of Homestead. He built an electric company and a telephone system (including Braddock), which became private companies. He was an outstanding electrical engineer, patenting a number of electrical controllers and other devices.

---

[6] Casson, 148

In the true tradition of the boys, Dinkey was part manager, part engineer.

There were a number of lesser-known "boys." One of these was David Garrett Kerr. Kerr came from Jones's hometown in Cambria County in 1882 to start as a laboratory boy in the Edgar Thomson Works laboratory. He had earned a degree from Lehigh University in metallurgy. He would work himself up to Chief Chemist and Superintendent of Edgar Thomson Furnaces. He was a true student of Charles Schwab and would rise to vice-president of United States Steel, a position he held to 1932.

Another of the "boys" was Thomas Morrison, a distant cousin of Carnegie from Dunfermline, Scotland, who started at Homestead Works as a machinist in 1886. By 1892 Morrison had risen to Superintendent of Duquesne Works. Morrison came earlier when Carnegie took over the Duquesne Steel Works from competitors. Morrison took the world furnace production record from Edgar Thomson Works and held it for four years at Duquesne. He was a great admirer of Bill Jones and a student of Charles Schwab. Braddock historian George Lamb noted on Morrison's leaving Edgar Thomson for Duquesne Works, "He was a strict, fair, and just disciplinarian, and when he left we find his men presenting him with a fine watch and heartily expressing their conviction that he had given a fair deal." He had achieved the hard-earned respect of his men through the sympathy strike for Homestead. In 1895, Morrison took over as General Superintendent of Edgar Thomson Works.

Many mechanical improvements and new processes, the most since Bill Jones, highlighted Morrison's administration. These inventions and innovations speeded up throughput by as much as 70 percent, smashing every standing mill production record. Morrison also followed up on the Jones theory of harmony of production, quality and safety. Following the

Schwab management style, Morrison implemented a Wednesday lunch meeting for his superintendents. This meeting is where process problems were worked out and improvements implemented. Like Schwab and Carnegie, he had a likable personality. Ultimately Morrison would become a director of both United States Steel and International Nickel.

Other boys included Ambrose Monell, who rose from metallurgical engineer to become co-founder of International Nickel. Along with him as founder of International Nickel was E. Fred Wood, who Schwab brought in as chemist at Homestead. There was also Torsten Berg, who started as a Swedish immigrant laborer at Edgar Thomson Works in 1879. Berg would invent over fifty equipment applications for blast furnaces, steel works and rolling mills. Finally there was Joe Schwab, who held positions such as superintendent of the blooming mill (Homestead), general superintendent of Duquesne Works and ultimately assistant to the president of USS. Joe Schwab would go on to form American Steel Foundries and become its president.

The greatest contribution of the "boys" was their new philosophy. They had developed a unique set of managerial attributes and personal beliefs that led to their many contributions. These concepts were a blended view of industry. Carnegie, Jones and Schwab as we have seen were major contributors to this philosophy but all participated. For example Corey was on the extreme right while Dickson was to the extreme left. Yet even these two extremes were blended through friendship and mutual respect. There are a number of these key beliefs.

1. Harmony In Manufacturing
Harmony was originally noted by Bill Jones as characteristic of efficient operations. Harmony is the integration of quality, production and safety. At its heart

is the idea that personal and organizational pursuits must come together to be successful. If for example safety is compromised to increase production in the long run production will suffer also.

Harmony of machinery and men was another part of this principle. The "boys of Braddock" were the leaders in the Industrial Edwardian movement that included Fredrick Taylor, the father of scientific management and industrial engineering. The focus was on the coordination of machine and man to achieve fast throughput. This is a break from the Industrial Victorians, who saw the secret to productivity in machinery.

2. Upward Mobility As A Key Motivator
The ability to advance based on performance was another fundamental principle of the "boys." Historian, Herbert Casson, used this analogy: "But it was a Napoleonic republic, this Carnegie corporation. Every private soldier felt that he carried the baton of a marshal in his knapsack, and the soldiers enjoyed the race as much as the general did. Never before, in so prosperous a business, were there so few stupid relatives and favorites in places of authority. Out of thirty-three superintendents, only three were school-trained. The others had risen from the ranks." Jones and Schwab, themselves had risen from rags to riches.

The motivational value of this approach was amazing. It did depend on good selection of men. Not all employees fall into this "theory Y" mold but that selection was part of the secret to success. Promotion was based purely on performance; age, experience, nationality and education were neither barriers nor limitations. Promotion from within was a "law." Many of the "boys" were running huge departments and plants in their early twenties. Alva Dinkey stated: "In steel making harmonious team work is essential to the best results and the natural leader therefore rises to the top by the general recognition of his fellows."[7] The boys realized that if you had any type of restriction to mobility, you destroyed a man's drive. Furthermore if you restricted a man's ability to rise in the company then his only alternative would be a union.

3. Men Have A Natural Need To Achieve
Competition was at the heart of everything. Even in their safety programs, competition was used for improvement. The boys placed achievement ahead of money and these were the type of men they hired. By doing this the money actually poured in. Money was a factor only in that it was one measure of achievement. Most of the boys were millionaires before age forty. Most of the boys were lovers of competitive sports and this was a source of this belief. The boys were also magical in their ability to tap into the natural need for men to compete. This understanding of the nature of competition helped them to develop some of the most innovative bonus and motivational programs ever designed.

4. New Technology Must Have Priority
We had already seen Bill Jones's belief in the technology scrap heap. New technology was a religion to the boys. Their Bible was the analysis of cost accounting. If technology could reduce the cost per ton

---

[7] Arundel Cotter, *The Authentic History of The United States Steel Corporation* (New York: Moody Magazine and Book Company, 1916), 119

of steel then it had to be installed or implemented. They were driven by product costs versus the balance sheet. This type of approach takes real courage. Carnegie had a strict policy that 75% of the profits must be put back into plant investment. The boys sent product costs (cost per ton of steel) into a spiral that made them supreme. These savings then fueled the payback on the investment. Morrison as Superintendent of Duquesne Works invested in a difficult economy in an automatic loading system for the blast furnaces that not only set world production records but also reduced pig iron costs by 50 percent. The end result was a 75 percent reduction in the cost of pig iron!

5. Shorter Working Hours Improves Productivity
Jones had been passionate that twelve hours a day was too much. The twelve-hour day, seven-day week and "the long shift" broke the spirit of the workingman and it was this spirit that was needed for productivity. This was another point where the Edwardian boys broke with their Victorian bosses such as Carnegie. To the boys, long hours were barbaric and reduced productivity.

6. Good Management Is The Alternative To Unionism
It was a simple belief that a union would never be needed if good management practices were applied. Bill Jones was both a manager and a union president in one person. With such a manager, the formation of a union is indeed restrictive. The boys were clear on their lack of support for unions. That hatred was not from a fear of higher wages but a fear of lower productivity. In fact Bill Jones believed in higher wages: "Jones's fundamental doctrine was: 'Low wages does not always imply cheap labor. Good wages and good workmen I

know to be cheap labor.'"[8] Of course in fairness, application of this principle requires a *good manager*. Jones and Schwab would over and over again fight Carnegie on his desire to cut wages. The boys in general opposed the Carnegie belief that wages should be tied to the economy and the price of steel.

7. Working Conditions Affect Productivity
Dickson held to the basic premise that working conditions and productivity were interrelated. The safest mills were the most productive. It is really a corollary of the theorem of harmony in the work place. Fredrick Taylor, the American father of Scientific Management, would prove the correctness of this view. Like so many of the "boys" concepts, the idea goes back to the work of Bill Jones at Braddock's Edgar Thomson Works.

8. Bonuses Must Be Tied To Profitability As Well As Production And Quality
This was a breakthrough concept of the "boys" that evolved from some of the early work of Bill Jones. The real modification came from that of Jones's student, Charles Schwab. Carnegie believed wages and bonuses should be tied to market prices and external profit factor. The "boys" knew that profits were a function of high quality, production and delivery besides market price. Again this view was really an extension of their basic belief in manufacturing harmony. Paying on production alone could result in actual profit losses. For example high production might be forced at the lost of quality. Paying bonuses on poor quality shipped product would ultimately (maybe months or years later) reduce profits through returned and rejected steel. In addition the

---
[8] Livesay, 133

workers would have been paid extra to produce this lower quality. On the salesmen's end the Victorian approach of paying on the tons of steel sold might also result in lower profits. For example the salesmen might offer more discounts to sell more steel while profit margins shrink. Some of the incentive systems the "boys" developed were a century ahead of their time. These sales incentive plans were based on profit margins, not on amount of steel sold.

9. Unions Inhibit Individual Performance
The hatred of unions was in a belief that unions took away individual drive and competition. The boys wanted to pay on performance, not on seniority. They feared unions would base wages and bonuses on a common basis, versus a competitive basis.

10. A System To Assure The Long Term Structure Of The Organization Is Required
Organization was at the heart of the boys' success. First they hired through a selection process that assured the main attribute was a desire to achieve. Then they backed up each job with men trained to replace their boss as he moved up. In this they build a self-sustaining organization from Carnegie on down. Schwab replaced Carnegie, Corey replaced Schwab and Dinkey placed Corey and so forth throughout their careers. The replacement went all down the line and through out the organization. In addition, this approach supported an important law of the boys: *promote from within!* Carnegie had taught the boys the importance of promotion from within. Carnegie often said "Morgan buys his partners while I grow mine." Promotion from within was critical to achieve the super-motivated

organizations of the boys. Carnegie taught further that promotion must be part of the company's infrastructure: "I did not believe it possible to found a really great business except upon the Napoleonic plan: every soldier carried in his knapsack a possible Marshal's baton. To bring an outsider in over the heads of men in service is unjust and should create a revolution.... Promotion from the ranks should be the motto."[9]

11. Safety Is An Integral Factor Of Production
Jones was the father of this idea so contrary to the thinking of not only the Industrial Victorians but also even today's managers. Dickson and Dinkey applied the theory with expertise. The production records increased exponentially as they improved safety.

---

[9] Krass, 321

Chapter 10

"The keys to success are industriousness and perseverance."
–*Charles Schwab*

The Industrial Edwardians

During the period from of 1901 to 1920 the "boys of Braddock" were responsible for forming three of the top ten corporations (USS, Bethlehem Steel and Midvale Steel) of the period, controlling nearly 40 percent of America's industrial assets. They would be responsible for the formation of another six of the *Fortune* One Hundred, including such firms as International Nickel, American Steel Foundries, Armco Steel and United States Shipbuilding. They would pioneer new metallurgical alloys in armor, aircraft and shipbuilding. Still it was their management style that had the greatest impact on American industry.

Carnegie, Phipps, Pitcairn, Thomson, Judge Gary and Frick were the Industrial Victorians who automated and mechanized the Industrial Revolution. These Victorians had made technology king. The Industrial Edwardians like the "boys of Braddock" were the lieutenants of these industrial founders. The Edwardians in the trenches found ways to merge man and machine into industrial might. Their rise to industrial leadership was not a paradigm shift or a breakthrough but a type of evolution. They worked hard and were loyal managers who patiently waited for their era to come.

Their real mark on industry would come not from technology and capital, but from human resource management. They would develop the concept of a corporate safety department and safety programs. The boys would help end the twelve-hour day so hated by Bill Jones. They would end straight time Sunday labor and the seven-day week. They would develop some of the first true pension plans. Their experiments in management would create ideas that would led to employee participation, gain sharing programs and collective bargaining throughout American industry. In process control, they would establish the first quality control departments and advance the science of inspection. On the technical and product front, they would revolutionize the building and construction industry with a lighter and stronger steel beam. These beams would launch an era of skyscrapers. It is estimated that by the late 1940s Schwab's famous new Bethlehem beam accounted for 80 percent of New York's skyscrapers. These new "I" beams would make up the superstructure of the Golden Gate Bridge in San Francisco and George Washington Bridge as well. Finally, they would set a role model for future managers.

The "boys" ruled the new corporation of United States Steel from 1901 to 1910. Charles Schwab and Julian Kennedy were the men behind its formation. Kennedy selected and integrated the plants that would make up the new steel trust of USS Corporation. Schwab served as USS's first president. William Corey followed Schwab as president of USS. Braddock boys, Dickson, Kerr and Gayley were key vice-presidents during the period. Alva Dinkey was president of USS's major division, Carnegie Steel. Joe Schwab functioned as assistant to the president when his brother, Charles, was president. Edgar Thomson Works was under two Braddock boys, Thomas Morrison and Charles E. Dinkey.

The boys had now come into their own. The Victorian ideals of Carnegie and Frick could now be challenged. Frick's control would not be missed but the paternal guidance of Carnegie would be. The lions, however, were to be tamed by a new master and Industrial Victorian, Judge Gary. Judge Gary's behind-the-scenes supporter was J. P. Morgan. The boys formed up on one side, informally known as the steel makers while the internal opposition was known as the "bankers." Gary and Schwab represented the two differing views of the company. Gary had the support of Morgan, which meant in the long run, Schwab could not maintain the presidency.

Schwab began to lose the political infights, making it clear that Gary was in charge. Schwab had too long been his own manager to revert back to a boy Friday. Schwab became disinterested and took up serious gambling. Judge Gary had opposed even the simplest forms of gambling, being a strict Methodist. It had been tradition to pay the directors of Carnegie Steel a gold twenty-dollar piece to attend the board meeting. The directors would match gold coins to select who would get the coins of those not attending. Upon hearing of the practice, Gary forbade it to continue. Schwab's trips to Monte Carlo made headlines in New York and ultimately hurt his career but they were only an excuse for Gary to work him out. The personal problems and lack of corporate control depressed him. Ultimately that depression caused health problems and even less time on the job. Schwab finally resigned in 1903 to go to Bethlehem Steel.

This resignation of Schwab and ultimately all of the boys was due to a major difference in managerial and business approaches. Judge Gary was a true Industrial Victorian seeing little need to motivate employees with bonuses, rewards and partnerships. Gary believed in a very rigid structure and system approach, which eliminated the human factor. Schwab came right to the point in 1902: "Judge Gary, who had no real knowledge of the steel business, forever opposed me on some of the methods and principle that I had seen worked out with Carnegie—methods that had made the Carnegie Company the most successful in the world."

Gary's view was to make his employees co-dependent on the corporation. Gary and Morgan controlled the history of USS Corporation and it puts Gary in a very favorable light. The boys, however, believed in giving the worker a path to independence. Still Gary, the politician, always put the views of the boys in a bad light. Homestead was used over and over again to discredit Schwab and his friends.

A year prior to his resignation, Schwab and other boys formed International Nickel. Fred Wood and Ambrose Monell headed this huge company. Schwab had brought University of Michigan metallurgical engineering graduate, Fred Wood, to Homestead as an industrial chemist in 1882. Monell had come to Carnegie Steel as a metallurgical engineer for Schwab in 1893. Monell would become Chief Metallurgist of Carnegie Steel and then assistant to Schwab as President of Carnegie Steel. International Nickel would become the innovator of a group of alloys that allowed for the development of jet engines and nuclear energy. This is just one example of Schwab's many contributions to the science of metallurgy.

In 1903 with the resignation of Schwab, Braddock boy William Corey followed him once again into the top job. Corey was the most removed of the boys. The Amalgamated union had been destroyed in United States Steel plants and the company now focused on what some called "welfare capitalism." This was Gary's grand plan to eliminate the need for unions. Stock and profit sharing programs were implemented in all the mills. All employees of USS were able to buy stock at less than market on the installment. In addition if they stayed employed at USS for five years, they received a five-dollar per share bonus. Still only fifteen percent of the employees participated in the plan. Most workers had little money to spare for investment. The goal had been based on the successful Carnegie model of making employees owners and ultimately capitalists but Gary had corrupted it to be used to make employees dependent on employment at USS. However, this new corporate environment world brought to the forefront one of the boys' greatest reformers, William Dickson.

Dickson was one of the first to see the weakness in this new stock program. Once the company deemed the stock program a "success"; it actually cut wages to "equalize" them. One historian of United States Steel called it "benevolent feudalism." That historian further recalled: "as soon as this plan was seen as a success—for more than twenty-seven thousand employees subscribed for stock in 1903 alone—another step was taken. The wages of the men were 'equalized.' The highly paid men were cut down from ten to fifty percent, while some laborers were raised to $1.80 and $2.00 a day. In some of the works the hours of labor were increased. 'I used to be able to make six dollars a day, working seven hours', said a Pittsburgh rougher. 'Now I can only make three seventy a day, working twelve hours.'"[1] They system devised by Carnegie and the "boys of Braddock" may have been philosophically in error, but Judge Gary's goal was control via dependence. The term feudalism is analogy for Gary's approach. Labor was not fooled by the positive spin of Morgan and Gary.

While Dickson fit in many aspects with Gary's approach, he was a loyal Carnegie man. In 1906 Dickson at the request of Gary became evolved with safety because of heat from the Chicago press. Dickson, in his rise through Carnegie Steel, had proven to be a great systems man. He had created a production planning system in the course of the confusion at Homestead. Corey saw him as the right man to put in charge of the badly needed safety system. Deaths in the Chicago mills were being highlighted. A *Chicago Tribune* article reported

---

[1] Casson, 251

that in 1906 forty-six men had been killed and "thousands" injured at the United States Steel South Chicago plant. This was not unusual in steel making. About the same time Pittsburgh's Jones and Laughlin mill had reported 80 fatalities for the year. In 1907, Allegheny County issued a report on Pittsburgh area manufacturing which was predominantly steel production. This report stated: "the Pittsburgh District annually sends out of its mill, factories, railroad yards and mines, 45 one legged men; 100 hopeless cripples who must walk with a crutch or cane; 45 men with a twisted, useless arm; 30 men with an empty sleeve; 20 men with but one hand; 60 with half a hand gone; 70 with one eye, and so on, 500 hundred human wrecks in all."[2] United States Steel was focused on the high cost of the problem. Dickson, however, was a true reformer in the vein of Bill Jones. Dickson was also a system man and industrial engineer like his friend Fredrick Taylor.

Dickson first developed an actual department to work with the problem. This department would later be seen as the: "genesis of the 'Safety Dept.' of U. S. Steel Corporation."[3] This group worked by training workers in safety and highlighting safety issues. Posters and bulletin board campaigns were developed. Accidents were analyzed by managers and preventive action designed. More importantly these changes became part of a managed system, which prevented recurrence.[4] By 1910, the corporation had over fifty employees working on safety. Dickson applied the basic philosophy of competition as well. There were interdepartmental and plant contests with personal awards. Dickson's system approach again showed results. The system

---

[2] *Steelmaking in the 20th Century* (Warrendale: Iron and Steel Society, 1992), 4
[3] Eggert, 44
[4] ibid., 45

is credited with reducing accidents by an amazing 43 percent in four years! Dickson's system was hailed as "a model for similar programs in many other firms across the nation."

Dickson had broken new ground in seeing safety as integrated with production. He proved that the most productive mills were also the safest. This was against the traditional thought of the Industrial Victorians, which saw safety and quality as trade-offs. It goes back to a concept of Bill Jones, who believed in a harmony among the factors of production, quality and safety.

Further down in USS, Dinkey was president of Carnegie Steel and continued to apply the success philosophy of the boys. Dinkey had followed Schwab and Corey to Superintendent of Homestead and finally to President of Carnegie Steel (USS). The Carnegie Steel administration of Dinkey went from 1903 to 1916. The achievements of the Dinkey Administration were an amazing legacy to the "boys of Braddock." When Dinkey had taken over as superintendent of Homestead in 1889, the journal *American Manufacturer* claimed: "There now entered that superintendency a man trained under four executives of such great caliber, and who, naturally of a reflective turn of mind and keenly observant brought to that office the noblest qualities of those that had gone before: the force and driving power of Jones, the shrewd tact and generalship of Schwab, the chemistry and detail of Gayley, and the sound common sense and business acumen of Morrison. In him each of these qualities of his predecessors still lived on in one master executive." Dinkey realized the importance of that training and grooming.

As president of Carnegie Steel (USS), he instituted a formal program to groom managers and back up the organizational structure. One of his trainees, who rose to Chief Metallurgist of USS, recalled in 1960: "Particularly interesting was Mr. Dinkey's description of some of the personnel policies of the

United States Steel Corporation in the early days. When the Corporation was formed, Mr. Dinkey had to select and assign men for plant operations. Backing up each man in the top supervision were three men preparing for the specific job. In addition, the policy provided for the selection and preparation of five younger men for future needs. In other words, behind each critical jobholder were eight men in various stages of preparation. Where could we find such strength and depth today?"[5] Dinkey applied the organizational genius of Jones and Schwab throughout a young USS Corporation.

Besides his organizational genius, Dinkey developed an aggressive safety plan for Carnegie Steel as well as fully implementing that of Dickson's. The following was said of his administration's record on safety: "One of the most prominent features of this administration has been the attention given to safety of the men. An account of the work along this line, alone, would fill a volume, for it is one of Mr. Dinkey's hobbies to make the mill safe. In line with this idea, the Washington Street tunnel [Edgar Thomson Works] was constructed during this year of the administration, affording a safe and convenient passage for the workmen of the Blast Furnace Department." Dinkey and Dickson became united in the importance of safety and its link to productivity.

Dinkey was also the man who saved Edgar Thomson Works from extinction in 1913. As Carnegie Steel, Edgar Thomson Works remained a Bessemer steel rail plant but the market was changing. Edgar Thomson Works controlled the market but started to lose market share in the later 1900s. The growth of the northern railroads with the increased loads of the railroads and higher speeds created a real challenge for Bessemer steel. Bessemer steel was naturally high in phosphorous and this element caused steel to become brittle in

---

[5] Earle Smith, *The Schwab Memorial Lecture,* New York, May 25, 1960, AISI

extreme cold. The Bessemer process was incapable of removing phosphorous and required the use of low phosphorous ores, which by 1907 were in very short supply. Companies such as Lackawanna Steel, close to the northern railroads, started to produce open-hearth steel, which could remove phosphorous. Dinkey with his metallurgical expertise saw open-hearth steels as the major future market for the railroads. Dinkey would approve the building of the open-hearth shop at Edgar Thomson, which would save the Braddock mill.

Dinkey's rebuild of Edgar Thomson would start a new series of industry records for Edgar Thomson Works. In standard railroad gauge rails Edgar Thomson under Dinkey's USS administration would make enough rails to circle the globe twice. In lighter gauge streetcar rails, Edgar Thomson produced enough to lay track to the moon! Dinkey would be the first to develop a mill metallurgical department, and he built a foundation for a major research center. Dinkey assembled the largest army of metallurgists on the planet to work for Carnegie Steel. These metallurgists would assemble what has been known as the Bible of steelmaking, *The USS Steelmaking Handbook*. The handbook even today remains the most comprehensive book on steels and steelmaking. It is used the world over.

With the two old Braddock trained chemists, Corey as USS president and Dinkey as Carnegie Division president, USS Corporation became the dominant source of steel technology. They supported the inclusion of metallurgical engineering degree programs at a number of universities including Layette College, University of Pittsburgh and University of Michigan, which were their major recruiting grounds. Schwab, Corey and Dinkey out of their simple, homemade Braddock laboratory had started the embryo of the world's greatest research center at USS Corporation. These three self-educated men would be responsible for the turning of the art of metallurgy into a true science.

Schwab left USS to take over near bankrupt Bethlehem Steel. After ten years, Schwab had taken Bethlehem Steel to the second largest steel company and the third largest company in the world in assets. Amazingly Bethlehem had hired Fredrick Taylor, the world famous industrial engineer, prior to Schwab to implement scientific management but it was a huge failure. Schwab's turnaround of Bethlehem was pure brilliance and a testimony to the Edwardian philosophy of the "boys of Braddock." Charles Schwab took the time to review and visit the mills and talk to the employees. Like his rebuilding of Homestead Works, the core of his strategy was developed with informal employee discussions. The challenge of Bethlehem got Schwab out of the personal depression that had dogged him for years as President of USS under Judge Gary.

Schwab the great competitor set clear goals for himself and the beaten down company:

"I intend to make Bethlehem the prize steel works of its class, not only in the United States, but entire world."

"What I am going to do is to make Bethlehem the greatest steel plant in the world. By that I mean the largest, most modern, the best equipped, the most highly specialized, and I fear the most expensive steel works anywhere."

"I shall make the Bethlehem plant the greatest armor plate and gun factory in the world."

Schwab further planned in the manufacture of guns and gun forgings: "To equal the output of Krupp in Germany and Vickers' Sons & Maxim in England."[6]

These goals were unbelievable for a broken-down, poorly maintained, cash-poor, iron ore-poor and over-manned company. Yet it was the stretch in these goals that was at the

---

[6] Hessen, 168

heart of Schwab's success. It was also a way to pull out of a personal depression. This for Schwab was no different than back in Braddock, when he wrote the record of the previous crew on the furnace floor, which produced a new record by the crew that watched him. What Schwab did was apply the Edwardian philosophy he had developed. First he sold off all the properties to generate cash for his plans.

Next Schwab took aim at the weaknesses of USS. These weaknesses came about because the company had scrapped the "scrap heap policy" of applying new technology. The reason USS had changed was that Morgan and Gary managed by balance sheet accounting to maximize stock prices. Gary drove the company based on the stock price, in contrast to the Carnegie approach of the company driving the stock price. USS had remained a Bessemer steel rail producer even though open hearth steel was clearly superior in quality for rails. The same company that under Carnegie had gutted a new Bessemer mill at Homestead to build open hearths was now reluctant to apply new technology. Schwab moved Bethlehem into a new product for them of open-hearth rails. Schwab filled his rolling mills to capacity and took huge amounts of market share from his old company, USS Corporation.

A metallurgical note may help here. Bessemer steel by its toughness, strength, improved impact resistance and ultimately lower cost had overtaken wrought iron railroad rails. We had seen that open-hearth steel was applied to higher quality products such as armor plate. Open-hearth steel had even superior toughness and impact resistance compared to Bessemer steel. USS had held on to the Bessemer process for rail making. Still Schwab, who was a student of the open-hearth process and had toured Germany, knew it was being used in German rails because it increased durability and life. The reason was the elimination of those old steel devils, phosphorous and sulfur. As usual Schwab demonstrated his understanding of steel chemistry as well as technology.

Schwab had defined two problems: "When Schwab took over active direction of Bethlehem in 1906, the company was operating under two handicaps: it had no cost accounting records [they had been lost in a fire] and its organizational structure was ineffective."[7] Schwab reorganized management to better coordinate sales and operations. Cost accounting and product accounting systems were put in place.

The close coordination of sales and production was a model that Carnegie had developed. This coordination had led to the first use of marketing in the steel industry. At Bethlehem, Schwab used his organizational genius to tie the infrastructure of the two areas together. This was different from the balance of the steel industry, which viewed sales and production as two distinctly different functions. Schwab actually invented the marketing department as a linking function and department.

Schwab's real impact at Bethlehem went to the heart of the boys' philosophy of individual motivation. Schwab set up bonuses for improvements in a) new production records, b) improved quality, c) saving on repair time, d) reducing waste of materials and e) reduction of second class material. This system clearly embodied the old principles of his mentor, Bill Jones. It differed from the bonus plan of Gary at USS. At USS, the bonus system was tied to corporate profitability versus individual performance. Another powerful feature of Schwab's system was that the worker was paid immediately. The Schwab Bethlehem system is also a historical mark of being the first gain sharing program ever applied in business. It also was an application of operational harmony, which put quality on an equal par with production that was lacking

---

[7] Hessen, 170

throughout American industry. Furthermore it won over the employees at Bethlehem, who had viewed him as an outsider.

Schwab, with the use of profitability bonuses, had resolved Carnegie's sticking point of the need to adjust to economic times. Carnegie held to the need for a sliding scale but that was clearly not acceptable to the workingman. Schwab started the rudiments of a system that would give bonuses in good times without raising the base wage. Wage increases lock in inflation and costs. Bonuses versus wage increases can at least modify the outside market pressure. Bonuses can be given when profits are high without building in a wage base that would create problems in bad times. The unions in the 1930s would reject this novel approach. Today, however, the idea is being reborn in the auto industry negotiations.

Schwab further extended his bonus system to superintendents. For the superintendent who could reduce the costs, he would share in the savings. His bonus system for salesmen is still novel today. Salesmen received a bonus not on the number of tons sold but on the profit per ton. This helped prevent the price cutting in the market place to increase order size. He also experimented with special performance bonuses in the machine shop. In general these bonuses inspired workers and Bethlehem's profits ballooned. The bonus system of Schwab differed from even the best of the Industrial Victorians such as Fredrick Taylor, who focused on piece rate systems and production. Schwab put the emphasis on quality, cost and profits as well as production. These are a visionary and harmonic approach even lacking in today's management.

Schwab as a young boy in Braddock had experimented with steel product properties. That early interest in steel chemistry had made him a great product innovator at Carnegie Steel. Schwab had learned product development at Homestead with his development of armor plate steel. In 1911, Schwab built a new structural mill for Bethlehem to produce a lighter open-hearth structural beam. The beam weighed much less but actually carried more load. It was the dream of architects having to build taller and taller buildings.

The new Bethlehem beam was to be based on a new process developed by Henry Grey of Ironton Structural Steel Company. Grey had discovered a way to roll beams directly from ingots, eliminating the need of an intermediate blooming mill. Schwab had studied direct rolling when, at Edgar Thomson Works, he was asked to study the "Duquesne" direct rolling of rails. This type of direct rolling would significantly reduce costs. Grey's invention, however, was going nowhere. Schwab while at USS had suggested the purchase of the process patent but was rejected by top USS management. Grey himself had found no interest in selling the patent. American engineers were skeptical and indifferent to Grey's ideas. Schwab, however, was a visionary with strong metallurgical expertise.

Grey's process was a direct rolling system, which required very clean, low sulfur steel. What most historians missed, but Schwab did not, is that to be successful Grey's process required high quality open-hearth steel. Open-hearth steel was what Schwab understood and he had built the best furnaces at Bethlehem. Without Schwab, there never would have been a Bethlehem "I" beam. Schwab developed the idea of combining his new open-hearth furnaces with the Grey process. The shape of these new beams resembled an "H" but eventually became known as the "I" beam. The Bethlehem beam would advance and revolutionize construction and allow for the modern skyscraper, as we know it.

Schwab had a vision that the "I" beam would transform the steel industry like the Bessemer rail had. Bethlehem's executive board told Schwab to abandon the project. Schwab would not give up. Schwab needed to build a new mill and he floated a bond issue to raise cash. Still needing more money to build the mill, Schwab turned to Andrew Carnegie, who backed loans with his USS bonds! Schwab's friend, Thomas Edison, was in awe of Charles Schwab in bringing the new "I" beam to market. Edison knew well that the real secret of innovation was not only the idea but also the perseverance to see it through to application. It was a quality they both shared and led to a great friendship. To bring the Bethlehem Grey "I" beam into production required a combination of financial, marketing and technical skills that only one man in America possessed.

Schwab highlighted his new beam in the building of Gimbel's Headquarters building in the New York. The architect of the Gimbel Brothers Store was Ernest Graham. Graham became a believer in the new Bethlehem beam and applied it to his growing Chicago business, including the Field Museum, Chicago Opera House, Merchandise Mart and the Insurance Exchange Building. These Chicago successes spread to New York in buildings such as the Metropolitan Life and Chase Buildings. Commenting on the success of the new beam, Schwab said, "We have found a steady demand for this new structural steel and the present necessity for rolling small sections handicaps the larger work for which the new mill was planned. No other concern can manufacture steel that way, as I have the exclusive patent rights for Bethlehem, but I have been agreeably surprised at the way this steel has found its place."[8] Ultimately this innovative steel beam of Schwab's would allow the building of the Empire State Building.

Schwab's success of the open-hearth beam did more for Bethlehem Steel than the Mustang did for Ford Motor Company. Carnegie, like Thomas Edison, found praise for this great and now forgotten architectural achievement of Charles Schwab. Carnegie went on to praise Schwab: "I think Mr.

---

[8] Hessen, 182

Schwab deserves a vote of thanks by Congress.... He visited Germany, and found in one mill the practice of rolling girders of scientific form. There is not a girder made in America that does not charge the customer for 15 percent of steel in that beam which is useless. The form is not scientifically right. Mr. Schwab is a genius. I have never met his equal." The Bethlehem beam was an architectural revolution started by Charles Schwab's organizational, technical and managerial genius. Schwab had done for the building and construction industry what Carnegie had done for the railroad industry. Schwab had proven himself Carnegie's equal and even superior, in that Schwab brought a technical understanding to the table that Carnegie lacked. Schwab's home chemistry lab in Braddock was probably the best investment Schwab had made during his career.

Chapter 11

"The thorough man of business knows that only by years of patient, unremitting attention to affairs can he earn his reward, which is the result, not of chance, but of well-devised means for the attainment to ends."

–Andrew Carnegie

Experiments in Industrial Management

In 1915 a number of the "boys of Braddock" purchased Midvale Steel. They were William E. Corey, who had been forced to resign from the presidency of USS; William B. Dickson, who resigned from vice-president of USS; and Alva C. Dinkey, who resigned from president of Carnegie Steel (USS). These were Braddock-born men as well (to be exact, Dickson was born a mile away in Swissvale). Midvale Steel would rise to become the seventh largest company in the United States. Midvale Steel would pioneer employee participation and ownership. It would develop a collective bargaining system and employee health care programs. Midvale Steel would coin the term "Industrial Democracy." Industrial Democracy would mean the full participation of the workers in the management of the company. Industrial Democracy goes even beyond the self-directed teams and employee participation teams of today. Midvale was to be fully democratic in decision-making. Midvale's approach would be in stark contrast to the paternal governance of Carnegie and the "Welfare Feudalism" of Judge Gary at USS. Both Carnegie's and Gary's system would not tolerate an active role of the workers in management decisions. The early Carnegie-Jones-Schwab system did contain the system rudiments of the two-way communication needed for future collective bargaining.

Midvale brought together the two philosophical extremes of the boys in Corey and Dickson. These two were also the best of friends with roots back to the coalmines of Braddock. Yet it would be these two unlikely managers who would lead the way to major labor reform. They would disagree but forge a new approach to labor and management. Corey would struggle and drag his feet but his friendship and respect for Dickson would allow the plan to go forward.

Dickson as vice-president of USS had started the battle for labor reform. His focus was the old twelve-hour shift that Bill Jones had proposed and tried to put in at Edgar Thomson Works. It was a battle Jones had lost with Carnegie and Frick. Dickson had protested hard that the twelve-hour day is counter-productive. Fatigue of the twelve-hour shift caused significant drop offs in productivity by the last four hours of any shift. Add to this the seven-day week and you have the human element far below its top performance.

Like Jones, Dickson lacked an active support of the early unions, which were more interested in wages. The union only saw a reduction in take-home pay for the worker moving from a twelve-hour shift to an eight-hour shift. Management on the other hand was focused on the need to hire more workers with a major increase in employment costs. Dickson and even Jones were looking at the problem from both perspectives as a labor reformer and productivity expert. Dickson's beliefs came from his own experiences as a youth in the mills. Actually Dickson had brothers in the mill as well. Strikers in an early Homestead labor problem had beaten one of them, Billy, in 1882. Billy was permanently scarred. Dickson was working at the Pittsburgh Headquarters of Carnegie at the time of the great Homestead Strike of 1892. The Headquarters office employees watched the battle at Homestead from across the river. Those days left a lasting impression on Dickson. In Dickson's view the real problem was not the union or management but the conditions of work. In particular the twelve-hour shift, the long twenty-four-hour turns and Sunday labor.

The eight-hour shift would have greatly increased the number of steelworkers needed. Judge Gary like other Victorians such as Carnegie and Frick had balked at converting to the eight-hour day. Even the union saw it as a potential loss of wages. The reasons for the opposition can be summarized:

1. The twelve-hour day was not continuous but had many breaks and slow times. There were stories of much sleeping in the mill during these slow times. These were built-in adjustments to survive the seven-day, twelve-hour routine.
2. The union would resist a shift to an eight-hour day unless the money paid would remain the same. Management would have to pay twelve hours of wages for eight hours of work.
3. Employment costs would soar. Management would have to increase the workforce by 25% to 30%.
4. Managers worked twelve-hour days so it is no more stressful than what management was willing to accept. This was clearly true in the Carnegie organizations but there was a difference for these managers. Carnegie managers were driven and highly rewarded based on their production.
5. It has been this way for over 30 years without outrage by the unions.
6. USS Corporation believed that a unilateral move would raise costs to the point that USS would lose market share.

Even with these objections, Dickson continued to fight on to eliminate the twelve-hour day.

Dickson even lacked the total support of his friend, Corey, who was president of USS. Corey was under the tight control of Gary and Corey could not afford to take on Gary, who was looking to force Corey out. Dickson tried to get the outside support of his old boss, Carnegie. Carnegie, however, stayed out of the argument because it was against his own theory of labor. Dinkey also sided with Corey. Part of the problem was that Corey and Dinkey were on Gary's short list to be removed because of Corey's social behavior.

While the press called Corey the "Iron Chancellor" because of his silent and secretive ways, Corey actually loved a party. Judge Gary was a strict Methodist who hated a party. Corey had left his Braddock-born wife for a world famous actress, Maybelle Gilman. It was a flashy affair making New York headlines. Judge Gary would not tolerate the publicity but the love-struck Corey carried on. One writer recalled: "The Corey-Gilman nuptials were discreet to the extent they were not held in Madison Square Gardens." The press was given the lavish details of $200,000 for the honeymoon alone, with a total cost for post- and pre-wedding events going over a million dollars. It should be noted that Corey had earned huge sums of additional monies from his chemical education in the Edgar Thomson labs. In particular he had developed a patent for hardening steel, which alone would have made him a millionaire. At one point it was even said he tried to rename Homestead Works, the Maybelle Gilman Works![1]

In March 1915, Corey and Dickson went to Europe. Both men were frustrated with the rule and philosophy of Judge Gary at USS. On their return Corey, Dickson, Dinkey and Monell built a steel syndicate to form a new company, Midvale Steel. Within a few months Midvale added the

---

[1] Holbrook, 280

Cambria plant at Johnstown. The United States shortly entered World War I, which put new ideas on hold.

After the war, Dickson would bring another failed USS proposal to the new company. The board of directors of Midvale had given Dickson the task of developing a plan for collective bargaining. This was a real break from traditional approaches but it did have roots in the informal problem solving employee committees used by Bill Jones and Carnegie. Informally the boys had always involved the workers in decisions. Schwab for example spent considerable time visiting employees in the work place in the rebuilding of Homestead and Bethlehem. Jones of course was an excellent model but some did lack the personality such as Corey to informally listen to employees. Dickson realized that like his earlier studies in safety and production planning a system would be needed. Dickson envisioned a system that would not depend on the good will and personalities of the managers involved.

Dickson posted a memo in the mills announcing collective bargaining: "Midvale was inviting its employees 'to cooperate...in formulating a system of collective bargaining, which will be of mutual advantage to the company and all its employees.' An employees' association, 'entirely in the hands of the men elected by the votes of their associates,' was to be set up. To get under way, the workers were first to elect a chairman of their meeting and a secretary to record what was done. They were then to elect representatives to a plant committee. The plant committee, in turn, was to meet immediately and select from among themselves a specified number of delegates to attend a conference at the Philadelphia headquarters of the company on Wednesday the twenty-fifth."[2]

---

[2] Eggert, 103

Dickson envisioned a blend of the old Amalgamated lodge system and the Carnegie department committee approach as a base for cooperative bargaining. Dickson, like all the boys, had a great dislike for unions, yet of all the boys, Dickson remained open to unionism at the end of his career. Dickson had that strong Carnegie view that good management could perform the role of the union in representing the workers. The issue was that in the long run you could not trust management without a structure in place. Bill Jones at Braddock had shown what type of management was needed. This was where Dickson seemed to have had a blind spot. Unions could be replaced with good management but managers were only human and variation would exist. The number and depth of "Bill Jones" managers would have required a very strict management hiring and training program even with a system in place. It only takes a few bad managers to cause a breakdown of the collective bargaining system. Still the Dickson model, had it been fully embraced, might have been an alternative to unionization on the scale that was to finally come to the steel industry in the 1930s.

Dickson approached the problem as he had production scheduling at Homestead Works and safety at USS Corporation. His approach was a system approach. Dickson defined the infrastructure of committees and processes to support collective bargaining. The grievance process started with the foreman and progressed to the superintendent of the department or mill. If this failed to resolve the problem it went to the local plant conference committee, which included workingmen with the general superintendent in the meeting. If still unresolved the dispute moved to a corporate conference committee and corporate superintendent committees where a ruling would be made. Ultimately the workingman grievance could finally go to the president.

The committee conference representative was to be elected from the workforce. Dickson believed these representatives would speak for the men "in all matters pertaining to conditions of employment, the adjustment of differences, and all other matters affecting the relation of the employees to the company." This proposal of employee representation in all matters was revolutionary. It was truly a model for Industrial Democracy. Corey and Dinkey remained cool to the idea but stayed with their old friend. This was the example of brotherhood among the "boys of Braddock." Corey had never seen the use of involving all levels of workers in business matters. Corey and Dinkey fundamentally opposed the inclusion of the low-paid "Hunkies."

Dickson's plan was extensive and multi-faceted. It involved ownership, community, education and fair pay. The key elements were:

1. An employee stock plan to promote ownership
This had been a strong belief of Schwab as a natural extension of Carnegie's successful management stock plan. Midvale Steel did institute a stock plan but profits were little if any for the life of the program. Wages were also too low for the average workingman to see the wisdom in purchasing company stock that was struggling in the market. Had such a program been in effect at Carnegie Steel, the impact would have been much different.

2. A profit-sharing plan
Profit sharing was another strong belief of Schwab and again can be considered an extension of the management plans of Carnegie. The lack of profits really doomed the program at Midvale.

3. A paradigm shift in management thinking
This was a major hurdle for Dickson. Corey and Dinkey were not true believers or supporters of the program. Dickson spent much of his time in trying to gain Corey's full support instead of unwilling approval. To Corey's credit, he had that Carnegie virtue of allowing a man like Dickson to pursue his passion. The boys knew well that these types of deep-rooted beliefs usually paid off in profits.

4. Employee education on a continuous basis
The employees never fully understood the collective bargaining process because it was so far ahead of approaches at that time. Carnegie was one of the first to realize the lack of worker understanding of economics and business. He tried to make his employee-managed store, the Braddock Cooperative Society, a training vehicle for the employees (like Junior Achievement today). Dickson used on-the-job training meetings to address the education issue differently.

5. A collective bargaining system
Dickson had the system. It was an employee elected committee system based on the early employee committees of Edgar Thomson Works. The system not only handled grievances and negotiated wages, but also gave employees a real say in operation management.

Dickson realized, as did Corey and Dinkey, that the success of this collective bargaining proposal would depend on educating the workingman. Dickson's plan was brilliant and was outlined by him in *System* magazine in 1919:

"The typical workman now has only the haziest ideas as to the nature and function of business he is in. Often he thinks of the resources as a kind of inexhaustible reservoir, from which the employer can raise wages as much as he likes by simply opening the spigot wider. Look into almost any workman's thought on the subject, and you will find something like that. Small wonder the demands of labor are often unreasonable.

The workman needs to know more about the actual problems of management. He needs to learn something about overhead, about marketing difficulties, about the dependence of production and production conditions upon marketing and the dependence of marketing upon economic production, about the numberless hazards and chances of loss, which his employer must face. He needs, in short, more of the manager's point of view. And the obvious way to give it to him is to let him have some part in handling management problems."

Dickson had hit on the core of the problem in American heavy industry, and not only would Midvale fail to successfully manage it, but a hundred years later industry as a whole as failed. I had the opportunity to manage in an experimental labor organization in the steel industry in the 1990s. Even with the huge and financially rewarding gain-sharing program (the average worker got $30,000 to $50,000 additional a year), still the workingmen and women did not understand and did not trust management fully. That was not their fault alone since we had several Victorians in top management, who continued to operate in backrooms, feeling the employees would not come to understand. The real issue is not in the education of the workingman alone. The issue is also the inability of managers to share in real decision-making. Dickson saw this inability clearly personified in his friend Corey. It was as Dickson saw it at Midvale; a never-ending circle of ignorance. Education of management and labor is the ideal that has remained unattainable both at Midvale and today.

In the end the great collective bargaining experiment died with Midvale Steel. The early 1920s brought a steel depression, which caused the end of Midvale. Corey, Dinkey and Dickson lost huge amounts personally as the stock fell.

Schwab at Bethlehem Steel came in as a white knight saving the company's stock value by buying Midvale. Corey, Dinkey and Dickson remained on the payroll for a number of years but moved to transition into retirement.

It is unfortunate that the economics of the times destroyed the most progressive approach to date for cooperative management. It was truly a design for Industrial Democracy. It was crafted in the foundations of the American democratic system. Still it would achieve the protection of the worker found in socialistic and communistic systems without the political baggage. It was flexible enough to calm the fears of the capitalists. It had the efficiency and direct problem solving of a two party system versus a three party union system. Edgar Thomson Works had shown that it could work.

Industrial Democracy was an achievement-based system, which was designed to advance the employee to the highest possible level. The only limit was drive and ambition. It was a merger of capitalism and democracy unequaled in any industrial setting even today. It was the answer of industries in democracies to socialism and communism. It was a real alternative to unionization. Gary's welfare management and feudalism left no recourse for the workingman but to unionize.

Even with his retirement, Dickson continued his efforts as a private citizen to change the steel industry's approach to labor. His ideas were taking root in the 1920s on a small scale. Henry Ford's new Rouge Steel plant decided to use a three-shift, eight-hour day. Judge Gary at USS Corporation held strongly to the need for the twelve-hour day and would not allow change. Dickson had become good friends with Fredrick Taylor, the father of scientific management, and together they suggested and wrote on many ideas that would ultimately be implemented in American industry.

Chapter 12

"Although I was the senior, still we were 'boys together' in perfect trust and common aims, not for self only but for each other, and deep affection, moulded us into a brotherhood. We were friends first and partners afterwards."
                                            –Charles Dickson, President CVA

Carnegie Veterans Association

The "boys of Braddock," as we have seen, revolutionized American industry. Their management innovations included the first to successfully apply industrial chemistry, cost accounting systems, and production planning in heavy manufacturing. They took the labor views of the Industrial Victorians such as Carnegie and became reformers. They were the first to fully implement safety programs and pension systems. They were pioneers in the development of municipal utilities such as electrical distribution. Their theories on human motivation were far ahead of their times. The developed innovations like profit sharing, gain sharing and employee ownership.

The first meeting of the Carnegie Veterans Association was December 18, 1902, at Carnegie's New York mansion at Fifth Avenue and Ninety-first Street. The mission statement of the Association was defined by Mrs. Carnegie and Dickson: "boys together in perfect trust and common aims, not for self only but for each other, and deep affection, moulded us into a brotherhood. We are friends first and partners afterward." This was truly a guild of extraordinary managers. They pledged to meet until the last one died. This guild had loyalty over the corporations they worked for. At the time of the first meeting they controlled the executive offices of USS Corporation. In the early 1900s, the boys controlled over 40% of America's industrial assets.

Carnegie was completely removed from the USS Corporation in 1901. Carnegie was, however, never removed from his "boys." He was for most of them a real father. When Schwab made the headlines for his international gambling, his biggest concern was to have to explain it to Carnegie. Carnegie scolded him over the gambling incident in 1902 and Schwab was hurt and depressed by Carnegie's hard approach. It clearly demonstrated the father/son relationship between Schwab and Carnegie. When Carnegie asked Schwab to come and explain, Schwab replied, "I have not as yet been able to muster up sufficient courage to come to see you. Your very severe letters to me and especially your letter to Mr. Morgan has depressed me more than anything that has ever occurred."

Schwab would also have informal meetings of the "boys of Braddock" including what he called the "class of '79"—a group of men who started at Edgar Thomson Works in 1879. Schwab hosted this additional meeting of the boys from 1916 to 1933. These types of side meetings continued throughout the years. For the many veterans in the New York area, they usually meet for lunch regularly at the Lawyer's Club.

What were the basic virtues of the Carnegie Veterans that allowed for such achievement and mutual friendship? The Carnegie Veterans had all the characteristics of a fraternity or a brotherhood. Their organization resembled a guild for managers. These bonds were formed by a number of industrial and business virtues.

1. Achievement

The single most common dominator of these veterans of Carnegie was they were achievement oriented. They were proud of the success of each other. Achievement came ahead of financial rewards and salary. Many times they would put their own money into the awards they used to motivate those working for them. Even their salaries were put in the perspective of achievement. Bill Jones's request to receive the salary of the President of the United States was not about the money but his mark of accomplishment. Jones in fact gave most of his discretionary money away. They believed in management by goals. Their targets were always the most and the best in steel production. Achievement was a religion for these men. They recruited, hired and promoted based on it. They invented the idea of benchmarking. They loved high pressure and performance environments. They were achievement oriented to a fault; often they failed to fully understand that some lower paid employees needed money from work for basic living.

When they found themselves blocked from achieving, Carnegie veterans became depressed. Schwab, when in the face opposition from Judge Gary, suffered from depression. To take away from them the opportunity to achieve, control and move up was the worst that could happen to one of the boys. They needed challenges and competition to be at their best. Blocked by Judge Gary at USS, they would one by one leave, not to retire, but for new challenges. It is probably part of the achievement-oriented personalities that drove them to a love of sports, cards and gambling.

In *The Forbes Book of Business Quotations,* Carnegie has one of the classic quotations, not surprisingly, on achievement: "Think of yourself as on the threshold of unparalleled success. A whole clear, glorious life lies before you. Achieve! Achieve!"

2. Loyalty and Brotherhood
Carnegie veterans had differing views, such as Corey and Dickson, but friendship and loyalty always was priority one. Many of these friendships were forged in their youth in Edgar Thomson Works. The veterans were a club that distrusted outsiders such as Frick, Gary and Morgan. The boys faced scandals, political fights, press attacks and corporate positioning but I could find no case of them turning in any way on one of their own.

This bond of friendship allowed for varying views to be maintained without any loss of brotherhood. There is no equivalent to the bonding of this group of men from childhood to death.

3. Creativity
Creativity was a fundamental characteristic of these managers. Carnegie, Holley, and Dickson were all writers as well as managers. Many like Schwab had a love of the arts. Almost all of them studied things like science and business on their own. They read and traveled extensively. Intellectual curiosity was part of every one of them. While they were loyal soldiers, when they came into their own as managers, their creativity blossomed.

4. A Genuine Interest in People
The boys enjoyed people. They loved to walk around the mill (with the exception of Corey) and talk. They listened and they were liked. They always had an open door policy. People always went ahead of the technology they invested in. They had all worked their way up through the mill and they knew first hand the problems of the worker. They were always giving back to the community and helping employees. People and

technology had to achieve a harmony. Over and over again, the boys demonstrated that they could run any piece of equipment better based on people. After Bill Jones's death in 1889, the *American Manufacturer* said the following: "He preserved in such a high degree the respect, the love of the thousands that were under him, and he deserved all the love they bear him and all the respect they pay his memory. No one more honestly and with more singleness of purpose strove in every way to help and benefit those under him than Captain Jones. Himself from the ranks of labor, he never forgot the fact and looked at all questions affecting the relations of employer and employed in the works he managed from the standpoint of both of these relations; and both employer and employed have come to realize that his judgment was in the main wise as they have always believed it was honest."[1]

5. A Belief in Diversity
Probably by today's standard the boys would not appear ultra progressive. Their time, however, was that of the Industrial Victorians, who segmented people into classes. Carnegie had been more enlightened than most industrialists of his time. Carnegie and his veterans were rooted in poor beginnings, which opened them to diversity in the work place.

6. Consistency of Purpose
There was a unity of purpose and belief. They had a management style they believed to be revolutionary and valuable. They wanted to see this methodology spread as an achievement and memorial to their beliefs and the old Carnegie system. That unity is found in that the

---

[1] Bridge, 106

Veterans Association was formed and functioned for so many years.

The boys loved Carnegie, but his harder Victorian views were either rejected or in many cases modified. We have already seen the modification of Carnegie's sliding wage scale and bonus systems. Carnegie was a bulldog for Darwin not only in the sciences but also in society. His Pittsburgh museum still today is a museum of evolution unequaled except by the British Museum. Carnegie translated that scientific belief into an operating belief in the survival of the fittest. His "Gospel of Wealth" is an economic application of survival of the fittest. This deep belief shaded his labor policy as well as his business policy. The boys, however, took more moderate view choosing cooperation over competition.

In general the boys worked together to improve on Carnegie's labor polices. Dickson led the liberal wing of the Association and had the most impact in the long run. Schwab more than anyone one else produced workable management models for profit sharing, gain sharing, bonus plans, and employee stock programs. Dickson fought the twelve-hour day until the 1930s even as a retired private citizen. As secretary of the Veterans Association and its poet laureate, Dickson penned many a poem. The association's press coverage in New York allowed many of these labor poems to get published, like the following:

> The Steelworker's Lament
>
> Mike Miller, on a summer's day,
> Raked the furnace, hot as say-
> The hinges of old Satan's lair
> And, as he raked, he tore his hair.

Alas for me, misfortune lowers,
I'm not allowed to work twelve hours.
No more at five, may I arise,
And rush with half awakened eyes

To toil once more, midst heated bricks
And molten steel, from six to six.
O woe is me, just eight brief hours,
And then, to sunshine, air, and flowers,

And wife and children I'm condemned.
I'm in despair. My life is hemmed
About with such restrictions, I
Might as well give up and die.

O Judge, don't leave us in the lurch.
Next thing they'll drag us off to church,
And make us list to hymns and psalms,
On Sunday morn, instead of damns,

And other expletives with which
Our bosses their commands enrich.
Our lives were quite ideal, we
Were very happy. Let us be.

And tell those poor romantic fools,
That if these new eight hour rules
Are forced on us, we'll up and strike.
We can't abide our homes, we'd like

To live in stockade, and then,
The Judge could, every night at ten,
Tuck those in bed who had a right
To this brief rest; kiss them goodnight,

And ask them if they'd been good boys.
But no such luck; Utopian joys
Are not for us. Misfortune lowers.
We're not allowed to work twelve hours.[2]

Dickson lived to see the twelve-hour day ended in the steel industry. Dickson continued to fault Frick for many of the problems of labor in the steel industry. On news of Frick's death Dickson wrote the following in his diary: "Death of H. C. Frick announced. A man I never admired. He was a cold task master and primarily responsible for the continuance of the twelve-hour day and the seven day week in the Carnegie Steel Company and U.S. Steel Corporation Mills." Dickson did live also to hear a number of admissions of poor labor management. One of those was Schwab, who at Dinkey's funeral in 1931 admitted: "Billy, when I review our past history, I am very much ashamed of the way we treated our labor. In my opinion, the working men have higher standards than the average of our class."[3] Dickson had remained to the end the conscience of the boys.

The success of the "boys of Braddock" was in managing people. It was all about people. Accounting systems, technology and product development were the result of the focus on people. It is the secret of the Japanese steel makers that overtook the U.S. in the 1980s. Historian Herbert Casson, said it best in 1907:

> "Here is the secret of the profits. It is not the high tariff that has brought the millions into the steel treasuries, although the tariff was an indispensable aid up to fifteen years ago. It is not the exploitation of labour, nor the

---
[2] Eggert, 159
[3] ibid., 165

plunder of weaker capitalists, nor the watering of stock. It is not primarily the possession of vast natural resources, as Europeans claim. The secret of American supremacy in the steel business is in the application of intelligence to every department. Here the inventor is appreciated. The ability to invent and to improve has risen to the dignity of a profession. The man who would have been a puddler fifty years ago is today probably a machinist or an electrical expert.

The Carnegie Company swept past all its competitors because it laid hold of these new forces of the nineteenth century. It focused the most energy and the most intelligence upon its business. It paid the highest price for brains. It hitched Ambition and Enthusiasm to its car."

The boys of Braddock left a continuing legacy in management methods and business. Their success can aid even those problems facing managers today. The steel industry of their times was every bit as global as today's. The Japanese rise to steel supremacy in the 1980s mirrors that of the boys.

Industrial democracy could have taken American business to new heights of competition. Their system was first a means to inspire any organization to compete and achieve.

The heart of the boys' view on the workingman was that the worker must be given the opportunity to advance and improve his skills. Carnegie had set the example with his libraries located in his mill towns. Schwab had built trade schools for youths to gain the skills needed in industry. Corey, Schwab, and Dinkey nurtured and finically supported many of the nation's engineering schools and chemistry departments. The Association also adopted Carnegie's creed of the necessity of giving. Where possible these donations went to schools, churches, science centers such as Buhl Planetarium, libraries, and recreation centers. They focused their giving and managing on improving the lives of the workers and their families. Nothing pleased them more than to have created a rags to riches story.

Bibliography

Baldwin, Leland. *Pittsburgh–The Story of a City*. Pittsburgh: University of Pittsburgh Press, 1937

_____. *Whiskey Rebels*. Pittsburgh: University of Pittsburgh Press, 1939

Bell, Thomas. *Out of this Furnace*. Pittsburgh: University of Pittsburgh Press, 1976

Boucher, John. *William Kelly, A True History of the So-Called Bessemer Process*. Greensburg, Pennsylvania: By Author, 1924

Bridge, James. *The Inside History of the Carnegie Steel Company*. New York: Aldine Book Company, 1903

Buck, Solon and Elizabeth Hawthorn Buck. *The Planting of Civilization in Western Pennsylvania*. Pittsburgh: University of Pittsburgh Press, 1968

Carnegie, Andrew. *The Autobiography of Andrew Carnegie*. Boston: Northeastern University Press, 1920

Casson, Herbert. *The Romance of Steel*. New York: A. S. Barnes & Co., 1907

Cotter, Arundel. *The Authentic History of the United States Steel Company*. New York, New York: Moody Magazine and Book Company, 1916

Davison, Mary. *Annals of Old Wilkinsburg and Vicinity*. Wilkinsburg, Pennsylvania: The Group, 1940

Eggert, Gerald. *Steelmasters and Labor Reform, 1886-1923*. Pittsburgh: University of Pittsburgh, 1981

Fisher, Douglas A. *The Epic of Steel*. New York: Harper and Row, 1963

_____. *Steel Serves the Nation*. Pittsburgh: United States Steel Corporation, 1951

Harvey, George. *Henry Clay Frick*. Pittsburgh: Charles Scribner's Sons, 1928

Hessen, Robert. *Steel Titan–The Life of Charles M. Schwab*. New York: Oxford Press, 1975

Hoerr, John P. *And the Wolf Finally Came*. Pittsburgh: University of Pittsburgh Press, 1988

Holbrook, Stewart. *Iron Brew*. New York: The Macmillan Company, 1939

_____. *Age of the Moguls*. New York: Doubleday, 1954

Kopperman, Paul. *Braddock at the Monongahela*. Pittsburgh: University of Pittsburgh Press, 1977

Krass, Peter. *Carnegie*. Hoboken, New Jersey: John Wiley, 2003

Lamb, George, ed. *The Unwritten History of Braddock's Field*. Pittsburgh: Nicholson Printing, 1917

Livesay, Harold. *Andrew Carnegie*. Boston, Massachusetts: Little, Brown and Company, 1975

Lorant, Stefan. *Pittsburgh: The Story of an American City*. Lenox, Massachusetts: Authors Edition, Inc., 1964

McCullough, David. *The Johnstown Flood*. New York, New York: Touchstone Books, 1986

Newton, John. *A Century and a Half of Pittsburgh and her People*. Pittsburgh: Lewis Publishing, 1908

Rupp, Daniel. *Early History of Pennsylvania and the West, and of western Expeditions*. Pittsburgh: D. W. Kaufman, 1846

Sanger, Martha Frick Symington. *Henry Clay Frick*. New York: Abbeville Press, 1988

Schom, Alan. *Napoleon Bonaparte*. New York: HarperCollins, 1997

Serrin, William. *Homestead*. New York: Times Books, 2003

Sharp, Myron and William Thomas. *A Guide to the Old Stone Blast Furnaces in Western Pennsylvania*. Pittsburgh: The Historical Society of Western Pennsylvania, 1966

Stubbles, John. *The Original Steel Makers*. Warrendale, Pennsylvania: Iron and Steel Society, 1984

Swetnam, George. *Andrew Carnegie*. Boston: Twayne Publishers, 1980

Temin, Peter. *Iron and Steel in the Nineteenth Century America*. Cambridge, Massachusetts: M.I.T. Press, 1964

_____. *Pennsylvania Notes*. Pittsburgh: University of Pittsburgh Press, 1940

Vogt, Helen. *Westward of ye Laurall Hills*. Parsons, West Virginia: McClain Printing, 1976

Walkinshaw, Lewis. *Annals of Southwestern Pennsylvania*. New York: Lewis Historical Publishing, 1939

Winkler, J. A. *Incredible Carnegie*. New York: The Vanguard Press, 1931

INDEX

ACHIEVEMENT, 208
ADDENBROOK, Thomas 80
ALLEGHANY VALLEY RAILROAD, 58-59
ALLEGHENY BESSEMER STEEL, 111-112
ALLEN, Ethan 48
ALLIANCE FURNACE, 34
ALSACE-LORRAINE, 109 141
AMALGAMATED UNION, 95 97 103 112-115 118-119 122-123 125 131 135 147 184 202
AMERICAN FEDERATION OF LABOR (AFL), 114
AMERICAN STEEL AND WIRE, 145
AMERICAN STEEL FOUNDRIES, 181
AMES LIMESTONE FORMATION, 7
ANDERSON, Col James 46 Library Inspired Carnegie 46
ANSHUTZ, George 35 48
ANTHRACITE COAL, 43 84
ANTI-UNION STANCE, By Jones, Schwab, Corey, Gayley 166-167
ARMCO STEEL, 165 181
ARTIFACTS, Ancient Indian 9
AUSTRIANS, 74 141 147-149 153-154
B-25 BOMBER CRASH, In Monongahela River 3
BALTIMORE AND OHIO RAILROAD, 50 67 71
BARKLEY, Mrs (Black Bab), Slave Of Wallace 30
BARNES, Phineas 9 68-69
BEAUJEU, 21 Capt Daniel 20

BEAVER WARS, Of Iroquois And Susquehannocks 9
BELL, Thomas 150-151
BENCHMARKING, 103
BENEVOLENT FEEUDALISM, 185
BERG, Torsten 173
BERRY, George Anshutz 48
BESSEMER, Sir Henry 52-53 56 59-62 102
BESSEMER AND LAKE ERIE RAILROAD, 71
BESSEMER PROCESS, 49 51-63 65 67-74 76 79-81 83-84 88 91-92 98 101 106 111 115-118 134 144 151 188-189 191 194
BESSEMER TUNNEL, 111
BETHLEHEM, 201
BETHLEHEM BEAM, 182 194 An Architectural Revolution 196
BETHLEHEM STEEL, 66 79 83 91 183 190 195 206 Founded By Schwab 106
BITUMINOUS COAL, 43
BLACK BAB, (Mrs Barkley), Slave Of Wallace 30
BLACKS, 119 141 149
BLOOM, 73
BODNAR, John 149
BOHUNKS, 75 86
BOLOGNA, Giam 156
BONUSES, 139 Tied To Profitability, 177
BOONE, Daniel 19 24
BOOTLEGGING, 154
BOUCHER, John 30
BOUQUET, Henry 26
BOYLE, Andrew 80
BOYS OF BRADDOCK, 6 65 78-79 89 91 101 103 105-107 109-110 113 128 132-133 138 145 159-161

BOYS OF BRADDOCK (cont.)
163 166 169 171 174 181
185 187 190 197 203 207-
208 214-215 Industrial
Lessons 136 Philosophy 173-
179 198
BRACKENRIDGE, Henry 28
BRADDOCK, Battle Of 21-25,
Importance In American
History 2 Artifacts And
Remains Found 24 68
Artifacts At Braddock
Library 156
BRADDOCK, Gen Edward 16
20-21 23-25 28 Death Of 22
BRADDOCK, Town Of, Early
Mill Days 144 Important
Attributes 31-32 Location 2
BRADDOCK'S DEFEAT, 17 19
BRADDOCK'S ROAD, 8 11 16
26 29 143
BRADDOCK ARTILLERY,
127
BRADDOCK CARNEGIE
LIBRARY, 156
BRADDOCK COOPERATIVE,
156 204
BRADDOCK ELECTRIC
COMPANY, 153
BRADDOCK HOSPITAL, 162
BRADDOCK WIRE, 145
BRIDGE, James 33 John 54 58
BRIDGES, F 80
BRITTLENESS IN STEEL, 44
BROOKLYN BRIDGE, 74
BUCKWHEATS, 100
(American Country Boys)
92-93
BUHL PLANETARIUM, 215
BULGARIANS, 149
BURD, 26 James 19 22
CAMBRIA IRON COMPANY,
40 42 52-53 56 60 80-81 84 87

CANADIAN PACIFIC RAILROAD,
74
CARBON, Removal 52
CARNAHAN, Robert 165
CARNEGIE, Andrew 7 24 31 45-48
50-51 57 59-63 66-71 74-76 78-81
85 87-89 93-98 100-101 103-109
111-119 121 123-124 126-134
136-139 144-145 147 153-154
156-157 159-164 166-173 176-
179 181-183 185 192-193 195-204
207-212 215 Character 168
Donations 167 Like A Father To
The Boys 208 Lucy 48 Mrs 207
Tom 45 47-48 57-59 61 67 View
On Labor 166
CARNEGIE LIBRARIES, 167
CARNEGIE LIBRARY, Of Braddock
162
CARNEGIE MCCANDLESS & CO,
61
CARNEGIE STEEL, 33 170 182 184-
185 187-188 197 214
CARNEGIE VETERANS
ASSOCIATION, 128-129 159 161
207-208 Virtues Of Members 208
CARRIE FURNACES, 127 155 163
CASSON, Herbert 77 79 164 174 214
CAST IRON, 35 37-41 47 57
Brittleness 38
CAST IRON FRONT BUILDINGS,
40
CAST IRON PIPES, 40
CATAWBA PATH, 8
CATHOLIC IMMIGRANTS, 141
CATHOLICS, Management Ceiling
Against 147
CHARCOAL, In Iron Making 5 33-38
41-43 48 76 83-84 162
CHARCOAL FURNACES, Wood
Required For 36
CHASE BUILDING, 195

INDEX

CHESTNUT, Used To Produce Charcoal 5
CHESTNUT RIDGE, 16
CHICAGO OPERA HOUSE, 195
CHURCHES, 142 148 First In Area 21
CIVIL WAR, 7 30 36-37 40 47 81 84 90 127 142
CLAIRTON STEEL, 163
CLARK, William 113
CLEVELAND, President 132
COAL, 5-8 13 29 31-32 34-37 41-45 48 50 54 84 120 123 131 133 141-143 156 163 169
COAL MINING, Chief Braddock Industry Prior To 1875 6
COKE, 35 37 41-45 48 50 56 58 71 79 95 98 116 121 123 133 149
COLEMAN, Lucy 48 William 48 57-61 67
COLLECTIVE BARGAINING, 201 204
COLUMBIAD, Biggest Gun During Civil War 40
COMPETITION, 175
COMPETITIVE ENVIRONMENT, 133
CONESTOGA WAGON, 13
CONNELLSVILLE, 34 42 44 50 133 142
CONSISTENCY OF PURPOSE, 211
CONSOLIDATED STEEL, 145
CONTROL VIA DEPENDENCE, 185
COREY, 159 A A 144 Family 142 J B 6 James 6-7 32 44 50 Maybelle 200 William 6-7 44 110 129 131-132 142 144

COREY (cont.)
160-166 168-169 171 173 178 182 184-185 187 189 197-198 200-201 203-206 210 215 William Career Details 164-166 William Personality 164
CORN, Ideal Crop For Monongahela Flood Plains 9
CORNISH, 141
CORT, Henry 39
COST ACCOUNTING, 66 75 90 175 192 207
COWLEY, William 45
CRANE IRON WORKS, 83-84 161
CREATIVITY, 210
CROATIANS, 155
CROATS, 149
CROGHAN, George 15 19
CRUCIBLE STEEL, 53-54 98
DAMASCUS SWORDS, 46
DARWIN, 212
DEATHS IN THE MILLS, 185-186
DELONG, Rev C 89
DEPRESSION, Of 1930s 6 63
DICKENS, Charles 37
DICKSON, 159 168 179 182 188 198-199 201-206 210 212 214 And Labor Reform 170 Billy 198 Career Details 169-170 Charles 165 207 Charles E 169 Developed Safety Department 186-187 Great Reformer 199-200 Thomas 6-7 32 William 6 91 144 160 William B 197 William Brown 161 169 William Great Reformer 185
DICKSON'S PLAN FOR INDUSTRIAL DEMOCRACY, 203
DINKEY, 159 165 168 178-179 188 200 203-206 214-215 Alva 102 109-110 129 144 160-161 175 182 Alva C 197 Alva Career Details 171-172 Charles E 182

DINKEY (cont.)
  Emma Eurania (Rana) 108
  109 Importance Of Training
  And Grooming 187 Rebuilt
  E T Works 189
DIRECT ROLLING, 112-113
  194
DISTRESSED STEEL, 120
DIVERSITY, 211 In The
  Workplace 99
DRINKING, In The Mill On
  Holidays 124
DUNFERMLINE, Scotland,
  Carnegie's Hometown 67
  156 172
DUQUESNE GRAYS, Baseball
  Club 88
DUQUESNE STEEL WORKS,
  111-112 172-173 175
DUTCH, 141
EADS BRIDGE, 57
EDGAR THOMSON WORKS,
  2 20 25 37 56 58-59 62-63
  65-66 68-80 87-89 91-96 98-
  103 105 108-109 111-116
  118 120 122 124 126 129
  134 136 146 152 154-156
  160-163 166 171-173 177
  182 188-189 194 198 204
  206 210 Building Of 143
  Managerial Mistakes 123-
  124 No Union 119
EDISON, Thomas 110 195
EIGHT-HOUR DAY, 82 85 94
  97-98 101 103-104 160 206
  Objections To 199-200
ELECTRIC RAILWAYS, 152
ELIZA FURNACES, 44
EMPLOYEE EDUCATION,
  204
ENGLISH, 74 119 141-142
ESPRIT DE CORPS, 99
ETHNIC DIVISIONS, 148

ETHNIC GROUPS, In Braddock
  Region 1
EUROPEAN IMMIGRANTS, 90
EUROPEAN MIGRATION, 11
EVANS, Lewis Cartographer 11
EXCHANGE NATIONAL BANK,
  59
FAIRNESS AND SAFETY, In The
  Workplace 160-161
FEDERAL STEEL, 133
FIELD MUSEUM, 195
FINK, Mike, Folk Hero Of Riverboat
  Workers 154
FINNS, 147
FIRE CLAY, 7
FIRST WARD, 146-147 152
FISH, 5
FLOOD, Saint Patrick's Day 3
FLOODING, 3
FORBES, Drives Out The French In
  1758 27 Gen John 26
FORD, Henry 206
FORD OF MONONGAHELA, At
  Braddock 8
FOREIGN LABORERS, 146
FORT COPELAND, 142-143
FORT CUMBERLAND, 11
FORT DUQUESNE, 16 20-21 26
  Burials After Braddock's Defeat
  25 Burned In 1758 27 Celebration
  After Braddock's Defeat 24-25
FORT MACHAULT, 1 16
FORT NECESSITY, 16
FORT PITT, Established In 1758 27
FORT PITT CANNON FOUNDRY,
  40
FORT PRINCE GEORGE, 12 14-16
FORTUNE ONE HUNDRED, 181
FOSTER, Stephen 31 William 31
FOUNDRY AND RAILROAD
  BOOM, 50
FRANCIS, Owen 155
FRANKLIN, Benjamin 11 16 38 46

INDEX

FRAZIER, John English Trader 11-12 14-15 33 Trading Post Burned 16 Nelly 15
FRAZIER'S CABIN, 20
FRAZIER'S TRADING POST, 34
FREEDOM IRON AND STEEL WORKS, 56
FRENCH AND INDIAN WAR, Beginning Of 16
FRICK, Henry Clay 7 44 95-96 98 112 119 123-124 126-131 136 138 144 146 168 181-182 199 210 214 Hated Unions 121 Tough On Labor 121
FRITZ, 92 106 George 81 83 87 John 81 83 135
FUR TRADE, Struggle For Control 10
FUR-BEARING ANIMALS, 4
GAGE, Lt-Col Thomas 21 Thomas 19 26
GAMBLING, And Racketeering 152
GANGS, 143
GARY, Judge Elbert 134 135 138 165 181 183-185 190-192 197 199-200 206 209-210
GATES, 26 Horatio 19
GAYLEY, James 101-102 110 125 126 182 187 160 Career Details 161-162
GENUINE INTEREST IN PEOPLE, 210
GEORGE III, King Of England 15
GEORGE WASHINGTON BRIDGE, 182
GERMANS, 74 92 97 100 119 141 147-148 Blocked From Using Bessemer Process 116 Immigration Of 1850s 141
GETTYSBURG, 41
GILCHRIST-THOMAS, Sidney 116
GILMAN, Maybelle 200
GIMBEL'S HEADQUARTERS BUILDING, 195
GIST, Christopher 5-6 19
GLASS MAKING, 7-8 29
GOLDEN GATE BRIDGE, 182
GOOD MANAGEMENT VS UNIONS, 176 202
GRAHAM, Ernest, Architect 195
GRANT, Maj James 26
GREASER BOY, 118
GREAT ARMOR SCANDAL, 131-132
GREAT LAKES, Iron Ore From 42 48 56 58 60
GREAT MEADOWS, 11 16
GREAT PANIC OF 1873, 63
GREY, Henry 194
GRIEVANCE PROCESS, 202
GUERRILLA, Tactics 19-20
H C FRICK COKE COMPANY, 123
HALF-KINGS, Iroquois 11
HALKETT, Sir Arthur 67
HARMONY IN MANUFACTURING, 173
HEAT AND BEAT METHOD, 51 53
HENRY, John 155
HERMITAGE FURNACE, 42
HESSEN, Robert 106 120 143 146
HICKORY, Preferred For Charcoal 5
HOLLEY, Alexander L 53 62 69 79 81 84 88 92 101 106 210
HOMESTEAD RAIL MILL, 113, 155 166 169 171 173 185 187 190-191 193 198 201-202 A Black Mark 129 Biggest Structural And Plate Mill 118 Carnegie Takeover Strategy 115 Converted And Rebuilt By Carnegie 116

HOMESTEAD RAIL MILL (cont.)
   Labor Problems 119 126 131
   Strike Of 1892, 126-127
   Structural Steel Producer 116
   Used To Discredit Schwab 184 Union Problems, 114-115 118-119
HORIZONTAL INTEGRATION, 48
HOT SHORTNESS, 43
HOT TEARING, 43
HOUSING, 152
HUDSON RIVER BRIDGE, 74
HUNGARIANS, 75 82 86 88 93 95 100 103 112 119 123 125 131 143 146-148 155 168
HUNKIES, 75 86 97 146 149 203
HUNKIETOWN, 146-147 152
HUNT, A R 144
HUSSEY, C G 47
I-BEAMS, 182
ILLINOIS STEEL, 111
IMMIGRANT WORKERS, Tension Between 146
IMMIGRATION, 143 Post-Revolution 27
IMPURITIES, 116 In Coal And Coke 43
INDIAN OCCUPATION, Of Monongahela Valley 8-10
INDIAN PATHS, 8
INDIANS, In Braddock Area 141
INDIVIDUAL MOTIVATION, 192
INDIVIDUAL PERFORMANCE, 178
INDUSTRIAL CHEMISTRY, 106 169
INDUSTRIAL DEMOCRACY, 197 203 206 215

INDUSTRIAL EDWARDIANS, 98 105-106 160 166 174 176 181 190-191
INDUSTRIAL REVOLUTION, 37 65 181 Carnegie Vets Were Heart Of 160
INDUSTRIAL VICTORIANS, 82 97-98 101 105-106 113 121-122 129 134 166 168 174 176 178-179 181 183 193 199 205 207 211-212
INSECTS, 5
INSURANCE EXCHANGE BUILDING, 195
INTEGRATED PROCESS CONTROL, 104
INTERNATIONAL NICKEL, 66 106 173 181 184
IRISH, 74 86 92 97 100 103 113 119 125 141-142 147-148 152
IRISH MOB, 152
IRON CHANCELLOR, 200 (William Corey) 164
IRON CITY FORGE COMPANY, 45 47
IRON INDUSTRY, Colonial 33
IRON MAKING, 33
IRON ORE, Insufficient Quantity 5-6
IRONTON STRUCTURAL STEEL COMPANY, 194
ISABELLA FURNACE, 48-49
ITALIANS, 75 143 146 168
JAMES, Thomas 80
JEFFERSON, Thomas 29
JEWS, 153
JOE BOATS, 7
JOHNSTOWN FLOOD, Jones Organized Volunteers 88
JONES, Capt Bill Great Manager 79 80 87-88 98 100 106 111 118-119 121 130 135 137 143 146-147 167 173-174 179 188 Bill 76 82-84 86 90-92 96 104-105 107-109 126 128 132 136 145 155-156 160-161

JONES (cont.)
168-170 172 175-177 181
186-187 198 201-202 209
211 And Safer Working
Conditions 90 Death 101-102
Desire To Break Records 90-
92 Effect On American
Industry 104 Fierce Temper
89 Hatred Of Unions 97
Keys To Success 92-93 99
Legacy 102 Managerial
Techniques 93 Motivational
Methods 85-86 Personality
And Generosity 85 88
Trained Charles Schwab 89
Treatment Of Workers 103
Character 168 Mr 69
JONES AND LAUGHLIN, 69 186
JONES LAUTH AND CO, 39
JONES MIXER, 91 104
JUMONVILLE, Coulon De, Killed 16
KAUFMANN BROTHERS, 130
KELLY, William 51-52 56 60 62 79 81
KELLY PNEUMATIC PROCESS, 51
KENNEDY, Julian 76 102 116 118 144 160 182 Career Details 162-163
KENNYWOOD AMUSEMENT PARK, 3 23
KENNYWOOD HILL, 23
KERR, David Garrett 101 110 160 165 182 Career 172
KEYSTONE BRIDGE COMPANY, 47 57
KINGHTS OF LABOR, 96
KLOMAN, 61 114-115 Andrew 45 113 Anthony 45
KLOMAN BROTHERS, 46-47

KLOMAN CARNEGIE & COMPANY, 48
KNIGHTS OF LABOR, 95 97 114 122
KRASS, Peter 68 90 112 157
KRUPP STEEL, 134
KRUPP IRON WORKS, Of Germany 59 116 131
KRUPP, 190
LABOR, Reform 170
LACKAWANNA STEEL, 189
LAFAYETTE, Marquis De 30
LAMB, George 1 151 172
LAPSLEY, Captain 80
LAUGHLIN, James 44
LEE, Charles 19
LEISHMAN, John 133
LEWIS AND CLARK EXPEDITION, Riverboat 13
LIGNITE COAL, 43
LIME KILNS, 7
LIMESTONE, 7 33
LIVESAY, Harold 121
LOCKS AND DAMS, On Monongahela 8 31
LODGES, 147 157 As Substitutes For Unions 119
LOGSTOWN, 14 34 Major Settlement In 1700s 10
LORETTO, Pennsylvania 107 120 143
LOYALTY AND BROTHERHOOD, 209
LUCY FURNACES, 48-49 61 70 76 109 162
MAGARAC, Joe, Mythical Gigantic Steelworker 1 154-157 160
MAINE, Battleship 118
MANGANESE, 56
MAYFLOWER, 142
MCCANDLESS, David 59 61 63 92
MCCULLOUGH, David 146

MCDEVITT'S, 108 145
MCKAY-WALKER FOUNDRY, 37
MCKEE, David 27
MCKINNEY, Mr 67
MEADOWCROFT VILLAGE, Ancient Indian Site 9
MELLON, Judge Thomas 7 32 37 129 Family 142
MELLON BANK, 7 153
MERCHANDISE MART, 195
MESTA MACHINE, 66
MESTROVIC, Croatian Steelworker 155
METROPOLITAN LIFE BUILDING, 195
MEXICANS, 149
MIDVALE STEEL, 181 197-198 200 205-206
MIDVALE STEEL AND ORDNANCE, 142
MILL TOWN, Characteristics 150 152-154
MILLER, Thomas 45-47
MINE DOGS, 141
MOLLY MAGUIRES, 103
MONELL, Ambrose 160 184 200 Career 173
MONITOR, Battleship 40
MONONGAHELA, Origin Of Name 2
MONONGAHELA PEOPLE, Mound Builders 9 Mysterious Disappearance 9
MONONGAHELA RIVER, Point Of Ford 8 Transportation On 31
MONONGAHELA STREET RAILWAY COMPANY, 153
MONONGAHELA VALLEY, Threatened During Civil War 41

MORELY, John 77
MORGAN, 165 178 183-185 191 210 Daniel 19 J P 63 102 133 135 163 182
MORRELL, Daniel 52 81-83 85-88 92 94 100 106 167
MORRISON, Thomas 67 160 175 187 182 Career 172
MORTALITY, In Steel Industry 90
MOSQUITOES, 5
MUSHET, 56 102 Robert 55
MYTHICAL HEROES, 154-155
NAPOLEON, 108-109 132
NATIONAL ROAD, 24 29
NATIVE, Wildlife 3-4
NATIVE AMERICANS, In Steel Industry 92
NEED TO ACHIEVE, The 175
NEVILLE, John 19
NEW TECHNOLOGY, 175
NEW YEAR'S EVE UPRISING, 125-126 162
NEY YORK SUBWAY, 74
NUCLEAR ENERGY, 184
NUMBERS RUNNING, 153
OAK, Used In Barrel Making 5
OLD MCKINNEY CLUB HOUSE, Restaurant 152
OLIVER, Henry W 45
OPEN HEARTHS, At Homestead 162-163
OPEN-HEARTH PROCESS, 59 116 118
OPEN-HEARTH STEEL, 189 191 Structural Beam 194-195
OPERATING DEPARTMENT, Developed By Dickson 169
ORDNANCE, Production 40
ORE DEPOSITS, 41
OSTERLING, Fredrick 120
OUT OF THIS FURNACE, (Novel) 151
PALEO-INDIANS, 8-9

INDEX

PASSENGER PIGEONS, 4
PATERNAL ROLE, Of Manager And Corporation 138 166-168
PENN, William 12
PENNSYLVANIA RAILROAD, 31 50 53-54 56 67 71 109 143
PETER TAR'S FURNACE, 34
PHIPPS, 58-59 61 109 181 Henry 45 47 49 62 110 John 45
PHOSPHORUS, 56 60 116
PIG IRON, 34-36 41-42 45 47-52 54 60 70-71 73 76 91 95 116 120 175 For Railroad Rails 37 High Carbon Content 38
PIG IRON KING, (James Gayley) 162
PINKERTON GUARDS, 96 124 126-127 143
PIPER AND SHIFFLER, 47
PITCAIRN, 181 Robert 45
PITT, William 33
PITTSBURG COAL SEAM, 42
PITTSBURGH, Importance Of Location 14-15
PITTSBURGH AND CONNELLSVILLE RAILROAD, (B&O) 50
PITTSBURGH AND LAKE ERIE RAILROAD, 71
PITTSBURGH BESSEMER STEEL COMPANY, 113 115
PITTSBURGH COAL SEAM, 6 43
PITTSBURGH FORT WAYNE & CHICAGO RAILROAD, 46 61
PITTSBURGH LOCOMOTIVE WORKS, 59
PITTSBURGH RAILWAYS COMPANY, 153
PLAN OF UNION, 16
POLES, 75 143
PONTIAC, Chief 19-20
PONTIAC'S WAR, 27
PORT PERRY, 30-31 111 142 154
POTTER, John 118 126-127 Death 129
POTTERY MAKING, 29
PREVENTIVE MAINTENANCE, 101 162
PRODUCT ACCOUNTING, 192
PRODUCTION BONUSES, 103
PRODUCTIVITY, 100
PROFIT-SHARING, 203
PROFITABILITY BONUSES, 193
PROMOTION FROM WITHIN, 178
PUDDLER, 39
PUDDLER AND HELPER, 154
PUDDLERS, 114
PUDDLING, 39
QUEEN ALIQUIPPA, Seneca Chief 12 At Battle Of Braddock 24
RACKETEERING, 153
RAGS TO RICHES, 174 216
RAILROADS, Importance To Iron Industry 50
RAIN FORESTS, Loss Due To Brazilian Iron Making 36
RATS, Considered Bad Omens By Indians 4
RAVINE DOGS, 7
RAYSTOWN PATH, 8 26
RE-MELTING, 41
RECORD BREAKING, As A Motivational Tool 99
REFRACTORY BRICK, 7
REMINGTON ARMS, 142
REVOLUTIONARY WAR, Battlefield Strategies 26 Importance Of Guerrilla Tactics 20

RINARD, John 80
ROCKEFELLER, 167
RODMAN, Capt Thomas 40
ROLLING MILLS, 40 83
ROUGE STEEL, 206
ROWE, Wallace 145
RUHR VALLEY, 163
RUSSIANS, 75 143
RYE, Used In Whiskey Making 12-13 27-28 32
SAFETY CONDITIONS, Improved 91 103
SAFETY INTEGRAL TO PRODUCTION, 179
SAINT CLAIR, 26 Arthur 19 42
SALOONS, 154
SCHWAB, Charles 54 77 89 93 101-104 106 111 113 115-116 118-120 123-124 126 130-133 136-137 139 143-145 147 154 159-161 163-164 169 171-172 174 178 182-183 187 189-191 193 195 201 206 209 212 214-215 A Visionary Re I Beam 194 And Power Of Competition 121 Character 168 Concept Of Business For E T 136 Depression And Health Problems 183 First Job 108 Gambling Problems 208 Generosity 107 Honors 107 Joe 160 173 Joseph 129 Keys To Success 107 Moved To Homestead 127-128 Personality 107-108 Rana 108 Rebuilds Bethlehem Steel 191-194 Rebuilds Homestead 129 Resignation 183-184 Steel Titan 105 View Of Unions 122
SCOTS, 142
SCOTS-IRISH, 74 141

SCOTT, 59 63 Col Thomas Director Of Pennsylvania Railroad 58 61 John 58 Sir Walter 46
SCOTTISH, 103 119
SCOTTISH DRAGOONS, 24
SCRAP HEAP POLICY, 191
SEARIN, William 119
SECONDS STEEL, 120
SELF-SUSTAINING ORGANIZATION, 178
SERBS, 149
SERRIN, 164 William 130 144
SHARPO, Irwin 155
SHIFTS, 150
SHINN, 90 William 61 75-76
SHORTER WORKING HOURS, 175
SIEMENS, Charles 116
SIEMENS PROCESS, 116
SILICA SAND, 7
SINGER, Martha Frick Symington 123
SIX NATIONS, Loosely Claimed Monongahela Valley 9
SKELETONS, Found On Battlefield 25
SKYSCRAPERS, 182
SLAVS, 95 100 103 112 119 123 131 143 146-148 168
SLIDING WAGE SCALE, Abolished In 1894 130 Described 119
SLOVAKS, 153
SLOVENES, 149
SMELTING, 34 36 41 50
SMITH, James 45
SNAKES, 5
SNAKING, Of Railroad Rails 57
SNOW, Caused By Steam Generation 74
SOCIAL CLUBS, 148
SONS OF VULCAN, 39 114
SPANG CHALFANT & COMPANY, 48
SPIEGELEISEN, 55-56 72

SPIES, To Report Union Activity 130
STATUE OF LIBERTY, 47 74
STEAM POWER, 74
STEEL MAKERS VS BANKERS, 183
STEEL PRODUCTION, Of Monongahela Valley 163
STEPHEN, Adam 19
STEWART, David 59 61 63
STOCK PLAN, 203
STOCK PROGRAM, 185
STREETCARS, 152
STRUCTURAL STEEL I-BEAMS, Used In Buildings 195
STRUTHERS FURNACE, 45
STUART, J E B 41
SULFUR, 116
SULFUR SMELL, 54-55
SUPERIOR FURNACES, 45
SWEDES, 92
TAYLOR, Fredrick 91 174 177 186 190 193 206
TECHNOLOGY, Investment In 138-139
TENNESSEE COAL AND IRON, 163
THE GOSPEL OF WEALTH, Carnegie Book 168
"THE STEELWORKER'S LAMENT", Poem By Dickson 212
THE USS STEELMAKING HANDBOOK, 189
THOMAS, David 83-84
THOMAS PROCESS, 116
THOMSON, J Edgar Edgar 31 50 57 61-62 67 106 109 181 Manager Of Pennsylvania Railroad 53 President Of Pennsylvania Railroad 56 59
TIN PLATE, 47

TITANIC, Steel Bolts Might Have Saved It 91-92
TOLEDO SWORDS, 46
TRADE, 13
TRADING POSTS, 15
TRANSPORTATION INDUSTRY, 50
TREDEGAR WORKS, 40
TREES AND PLANTS, 5
TUBAL-CAIN, The Steel Angel 154
TURTLE CREEK, Town Of 31
TWELVE-HOUR DAY, 170 175 181 198 214
TWELVE-HOUR SHIFT, 130
UNION MILLS, 57
UNIONS, Hated By Jones 94
UNITED STATES SHIPBUILDING, 181
UNITED STATES STEEL, 6 25 50 54 66 77 80 102 110-111 133-134 136 145-146 161 163 165 181-182 184-185 187-192 194 197-198 200-202 206-209 214 Founded By Schwab 106
UPWARD MOBILITY, 174
USS, (See United States Steel Corporation)
VANDERBILT, 167
VICKERS' SONS & MAXIM, 190
VIRGINIA PATH, 11
VULCAN LODGES, 39
WALLACE, George 30 Owner Of Braddock's Field 28
WAR OF 1812, 29
WARD, Capt E B 52 79 81
WARRIORS PATH, 8
WASHINGTON, George 1 3 8 11-12 14 19-21 23-24 26 30-31 46 74 154 And Whiskey Rebellion 29 At Logstown 10 Heroism At Battle Of Braddock 22 Surrender At Fort Necessity 16 Lawrence (Brother Of George) 6

WAYNE, Mad Anthony 34
WEIR, Ernest Tener 145
WEIRTON, West Virginia 145
WEIRTON STEEL, 145
WELFARE CAPITALISM, 134
WELFARE FEUDALISM, 197
WELSH, 74 96-97 100 103 113 119 141-142 148
WESTERN MARYLAND RAILROAD, 71
WHISKEY, 34
WHISKEY REBELLION, Of 1794 27-29 124
WHISKEY TAX, 28 141
WHITWALL, Mr 49
WIDOW MEYER'S HOTEL, Where Washington Stopped 31
WILKINS, Gen John 28
WILSON, James 45
WOOD, E Fred 173 Fred 184
WORKING CONDITIONS, 199 And Productivity 177
WORKING HARMONY, 104
WORLD WAR I, 201
WROUGHT IRON, High Impact Strength 39
YELLOW DOG CONTRACTS, 95 113
YOUNG GENIUSES, 160-161

www.ingramcontent.com/pod-product-compliance
Lightning Source LLC
Chambersburg PA
CBHW070734160426
43192CB00009B/1432